Illumine
My Spirit

Illumine
My Spirit

Bahá'í Prayers and Meditations for Women

Compiled by Bahá'í Publishing

Bahá'í
PUBLISHING
Wilmette, Illinois

Bahá'í Publishing
415 Linden Avenue, Wilmette, Illinois 60091-2844

Copyright © 2008 by the National Spiritual Assembly of
the Bahá'ís of the United States

11   10   09   4   3   2

Library of Congress Cataloging-in-Publication Data

Illumine my spirit : Bahá'í prayers and meditations for
women / compiled by Bahá'í Publishing.
   p. cm.
 Includes bibliographical references and (p.   )
index.
 ISBN-13: 978-1-931847-57-5 (pbk. : alk. paper)
 ISBN-10: 1-931847-57-6 (pbk. : alk. paper)   1.
Bahai women—Prayers and devotions. 2. Bahai
Faith—Prayers and devotions.

 BP380I45 2008
 297.9'3433082—dc22

                              2008022198

Cover design by Misha Maynerick
Book design by Suni D. Hannan

Contents

Introduction

Women have a special role to play in the world today. They often shoulder—sometimes single-handedly—the critical responsibility of caring for their children while actively participating in education, work, and the public sphere. Because of the numerous demands placed on them, women frequently find themselves juggling the different roles of wife, mother, and worker. In spite of the undeniable contributions they have made to society, women today still struggle—both at work and at home—for equality with men.

The unique abilities and contributions that women offer are recognized in the Bahá'í writings. Bahá'u'lláh taught that women and men are created equal and that motherhood and the education of children are of the utmost importance. The Bahá'í writings say that until full equality between women and men is realized, true progress for the human race will not be accomplished. The Bahá'í writings also explain that mothers are the first teachers of children and it is essential that they impart to their children what it means to have high morals and an upright character, and to exhibit the virtues of God to all of humankind. The spiritual guidance offered through the Bahá'í writings is particularly suited to the needs of women in contemporary society. As the most recent of the world's religions, the Bahá'í Faith offers social and spiritual principles and a unique insight attuned to the requirements of today's world.

The Bahá'í Faith is an independent world religion that began in 1844 in Persia (present-day Iran). Since its inception the Bahá'í Faith has spread to 235 nations and territories and has been accepted by more than five million people. The Bahá'í Faith was founded by Bahá'u'lláh, Whose name means "the glory of God." Bahá'ís believe that there is only one God, that all the major world religions come from God, and that all the members of the human race are essentially members of one family. Bahá'ís strive to eliminate all forms of prejudice and believe that people of all races, nations, social status, and religious backgrounds are equal in the sight of God. The Bahá'í Faith also teaches that each individual is responsible for the independent investigation of truth, that science and religion are in harmony, and that men and women are equal in the sight of God.

Before Bahá'u'lláh revealed His mission, His coming was announced by another Prophet known as the Báb, Whose name means "the gate." The Báb foretold the coming of a new Prophet of God, Whom He referred to as "Him Whom God shall make manifest." The one to Whom He referred would fulfill the prophecies of all the religious traditions of the past and usher in a new age of peace and maturity for the human race. The Báb was martyred in 1850 by the Persian government for spreading the message that the appearance of a new Manifestation of God was imminent.

Following the martyrdom of the Báb, Bahá'u'lláh continued to spread the Báb's message and prepare the Báb's followers for the coming of the Promised One. Bahá'u'lláh did not reveal His station as "Him Whom God shall make manifest" until 1863. Throughout His life Bahá'u'lláh was persecuted, imprisoned, and exiled for His teachings. He passed away in 1892 and in His Will and Testament appointed His eldest son, 'Abdu'l-Bahá, whose name means "servant of the glory," as His successor.

Throughout his life 'Abdu'l-Bahá worked unceasingly to elucidate the teachings of Bahá'u'lláh for the new and growing Bahá'í community. Before his passing in 1921, 'Abdu'l-Bahá appointed his grandson Shoghi Effendi as the Guardian of the Bahá'í Faith. Shoghi Effendi was given the authority to interpret the sacred texts written by Bahá'u'lláh, the Báb, and 'Abdu'l-Bahá and to lead the

Bahá'í community. He served as the Guardian of the Faith until his passing in 1957.

After the passing of the Guardian, the Universal House of Justice, the supreme governing and legislative body of the Bahá'í Faith, was established. The Universal House of Justice is made up of nine members and is elected by the Bahá'ís of the world every five years. It gives spiritual guidance to the worldwide Bahá'í community and directs its administrative activities.

This compilation includes prayers and writings from Bahá'u'lláh, the Báb, and 'Abdu'l-Bahá, as well as the writings of the Universal House of Justice and Bahíyyih Khánum. Bahíyyih Khánum is the daughter of Bahá'u'lláh and is considered an outstanding heroine of the Bahá'í Faith for her unwavering support of her father in the face of persecution and for her service to the Bahá'í Faith throughout her life.

In the passages included in this compilation, a few terms may require clarification. These include *handmaidens, bondswoman, daughter of the Kingdom, leaf, and leaves.* All of these terms refer to the female followers of Bahá'u'lláh, or Bahá'ís. Some of the selections particularly refer to female believers, while others are written for a general audience. In regard to the writings for a general audience, some selections use male pronouns to refer to all of humanity. These passages have been translated from Persian or Arabic. In the original languages, pronouns were used that have no gender; however, when translated into English, male pronouns were applied.

The prayers and meditations included in this book cover a wide variety of topics that will speak to women for whatever need arises. It is hoped that this compilation will serve as a source of guidance and inspiration for women from all religious backgrounds, cultures, and traditions.

Assistance

1

Magnified be Thy name, O Thou in Whose grasp are the reins of the souls of all them that have recognized Thee, and in Whose right hand are the destinies of all that are in heaven and all that are on earth! Thou doest, through the power of Thy might, what Thou willest, and ordainest, by an act of Thy volition, what Thou pleasest. The will of the most resolute of men is as nothing when compared with the compelling evidences of Thy will, and the determination of the most inflexible among Thy creatures is dissipated before the manifold revelations of Thy purpose.

Thou art He Who, through a word of Thy mouth, hath so enravished the hearts of Thy chosen ones that they have, in their love for Thee, detached themselves from all except Thyself, and laid down their lives and sacrificed their souls in Thy path, and borne, for Thy sake, what none of Thy creatures hath borne.

I am one of Thy handmaidens, O my Lord! I have turned my face towards the habitation of Thy mercy, and have sought the wonders of Thy manifold favors, inasmuch as all the members of my body proclaim Thee to be the All-Bounteous, He Whose grace is immense.

O Thou Whose face is the object of my adoration, Whose beauty is my sanctuary, Whose court is my goal, Whose remembrance is my wish, Whose affection is my solace, Whose love is my begetter, Whose praise is my companion, Whose nearness is my hope, Whose presence is my greatest longing and supreme aspiration! Disappoint me not, I entreat Thee, by withholding from me the things Thou didst ordain for the chosen ones among Thy handmaidens, and supply me with the good of this world and of the world to come.

Thou art, verily, the Lord of creation. No God is there beside Thee, the Ever-Forgiving, the Most Bountiful.

—*Bahá'u'lláh*

2

I implore Thee to assist me and them that love me to magnify Thy Word, and to endow us with such strength that the ills of this world and its tribulations will be powerless to hinder us from remembering Thee and from extolling Thy virtues. Powerful art Thou to do all things; resplendent art Thou above all things.

—*Bahá'u'lláh*

3

O Thou kind God! In the utmost state of humility and submission do we entreat and supplicate at Thy threshold, seeking Thine endless confirmations and illimitable assistance. O Thou Lord! Regenerate these souls, and confer upon them a new life. Animate the spirits, inform the hearts, open the eyes, and make the ears attentive. From Thine ancient treasury confer a new being and animus, and from Thy preexistent abode assist them to attain to new confirmations.

O God! Verily, the world is in need of reformation. Bestow upon it a new existence. Give it newness of thoughts, and reveal unto it heavenly sciences. Breathe into it a fresh spirit, and grant unto it a holier and higher purpose.

O God! Verily, Thou hast made this century radiant, and in it Thou hast manifested Thy merciful effulgence. Thou hast effaced the darkness of superstitions and permitted the light of assurance to shine. O God! Grant that these servants may be acceptable at Thy threshold. Reveal a new heaven, and spread out a new earth for habitation. Let a new Jerusalem descend from on high. Bestow new thoughts, new life upon mankind. Endow souls with new perceptions, and confer upon them new virtues. Verily, Thou art the Almighty, the Powerful. Thou art the Giver, the Generous.

—'Abdu'l-Bahá

4

O Lord! We are weak; strengthen us. O God! We are ignorant; make us knowing. O Lord! We are poor; make us wealthy. O God! We are dead; quicken us. O Lord! We are humiliation itself; glorify us in Thy Kingdom. If Thou dost assist us, O Lord, we shall become as scintillating stars. If Thou dost not assist us, we shall become lower than the earth. O Lord! Strengthen us. O God! Confer victory upon us. O God! Enable us to conquer self and overcome desire. O Lord! Deliver us from the bondage of the material world. O Lord! Quicken us through the breath of the Holy Spirit in order that we may arise to serve Thee, engage in worshipping Thee and exert ourselves in Thy Kingdom with the utmost sincerity. O Lord, Thou art powerful. O God, Thou art forgiving. O Lord, Thou art compassionate.

—'Abdu'l-Bahá

5

O God, my God! Thou art my Hope and my Beloved, my highest Aim and Desire! With great humbleness and entire devotion I pray to Thee to make me a minaret of Thy love in Thy land, a lamp of Thy knowledge among Thy creatures, and a banner of divine bounty in Thy dominion.

Number me with such of Thy servants as have detached themselves from everything but Thee, have sanctified themselves from the transitory things of this world, and have freed themselves from the promptings of the voicers of idle fancies.

Let my heart be dilated with joy through the spirit of confirmation from Thy kingdom, and brighten my eyes by beholding the hosts of divine assistance descending successively upon me from the kingdom of Thine omnipotent glory.

Thou art, in truth, the Almighty, the All-Glorious, the All-Powerful.

—'Abdu'l-Bahá

Certitude

1

Thou beholdest, O my God, how every bone in my body soundeth like a pipe with the music of Thine inspiration, revealing the signs of Thy oneness and the clear tokens of Thy unity. I entreat Thee, O my God, by Thy Name which irradiateth all things, to raise up such servants as shall incline their ears to the voice of the melodies that hath ascended from the right hand of the throne of Thy glory. Make them, then, to quaff from the hand of Thy grace the wine of Thy mercy, that it may assure their hearts, and cause them to turn away from the left hand of idle fancies and vain imaginings to the right hand of confidence and certitude.

Now that Thou hast guided them unto the door of Thy grace, O my Lord, cast them not away, by Thy bounty; and now that Thou hast summoned them unto the horizon of Thy Cause, keep them not back from Thee, by Thy graciousness and favor. Powerful art Thou to do as Thou pleasest. No God is there but Thee, the Omniscient, the All-Informed.

—Bahá'u'lláh

2

Nowhere doth your true and abiding glory reside except in your firm adherence unto the precepts of God, your wholehearted observance of His laws, your resolution to see that they do not remain unenforced, and to pursue steadfastly the right course.

—*Bahá'u'lláh*

3

I beseech Thee, O God of bounty and King of all created things, to guard Thy servants from the imaginations which their hearts may devise. Raise them up, then, to such heights that their footsteps may slip not in the face of the evidences of Thy handiwork, which the manifold exigencies of Thy wisdom have ordained, and whose secrets Thou hast hid from the face of Thy people and Thy creatures. Withhold them not, O my Lord, from the ocean of Thy knowledge, neither do Thou deprive them of what Thou didst destine for such of Thy chosen ones as have near access to Thee, and those of Thy trusted ones as are wholly devoted to Thy Self. Supply them, then, from Thy sea of certainty with what will calm the agitation of their hearts. Turn, O Lord my God, the darkness of their fancies into the brightness of certitude, and cause them to arise, and to walk steadfastly in Thy straight Path, that haply Thy Book may not hinder them from recognizing Him Who is its Revealer, and Thy names from acknowledging the One Who is their Creator, and their Provider, and their Origin, and their King, and their Begetter, and their Destroyer, and their Glorifier, and their Abaser, and their Governor, and the Sovereign Protector of their Bearers.

—Bahá'u'lláh

4

Do Thou ordain for me through Thy most exalted Pen, O my Lord, the good of this world and of the next. I testify that within Thy grasp are held the reins of all things. Thou changest them as Thou pleasest. No God is there save Thee, the Strong, the Faithful.

Thou art He Who changeth through His bidding abasement into glory, and weakness into strength, and powerlessness into might, and fear into calm, and doubt into certainty. No God is there but Thee, the Mighty, the Beneficent.

Thou disappointest no one who hath sought Thee, nor dost Thou keep back from Thee any one who hath desired Thee. Ordain Thou for me what becometh the heaven of Thy generosity, and the ocean of Thy bounty. Thou art, verily, the Almighty, the Most Powerful.

—Bahá'u'lláh

5

The effulgence of the rays of the Sun of Truth is abundant and the favors of the Blessed Beauty surround the women believers and the handmaidens who have attained unto certitude. At every moment a bounteous bestowal is revealed. The handmaidens of the Merciful should seize the opportunities afforded in these days. Each one should strive to draw nigh unto the divine Threshold and seek bounties from the Source of existence. She should attain such a state and be confirmed with such a power as to make, with but the utterance of one word, a lowly person to be held in reverence, initiate him who is deprived into the world of the spirit, impart hope to the despondent, endow the portionless one with a share of the great bestowal, and confer knowledge and insight upon the ignorant and the blind, and alertness and vigilance on the indolent and heedless. This is the attribute of the handmaidens of the Merciful. This is the characteristic of the bondsmaids of God's Threshold.

—'Abdu'l-Bahá

6

O Thou kind Lord! Bestow heavenly confirmation upon this daughter of the Kingdom, and graciously aid her that she may remain firm and steadfast in Thy Cause and that she may, even as a nightingale of the rose garden of mysteries, warble melodies in the Abhá Kingdom* in the most wondrous tones, thereby bringing happiness to everyone. Make her exalted among the daughters of the kingdom and enable her to attain life eternal.

Thou art the Bestower, the All-Loving.

—'Abdu'l-Bahá

7

O thou dear handmaid of God! Thy letter hath been received and its contents noted. Thou didst ask for a rule whereby to guide thy life.

Believe thou in God, and keep thine eyes fixed upon the exalted Kingdom; be thou enamored of the Abhá Beauty;† stand thou firm in the Covenant;‡ yearn thou to ascend into the Heaven of the Universal Light. Be thou severed from this world, and reborn through the sweet scents of holiness that blow from the realm of the All-Highest. Be thou a summoner to love, and be thou kind to

---

* *The Most Glorious Kingdom*: the spiritual world beyond this world.

†A translation of *Jamál-i-Abhá,* a title of Bahá'u'lláh.

‡ The binding agreement between God and humanity that God will provide guidance to humankind and that humankind will accept it.

17

all the human race. Love thou the children of men and share in their sorrows. Be thou of those who foster peace. Offer thy friendship, be worthy of trust. Be thou a balm to every sore, be thou a medicine for every ill. Bind thou the souls together. Recite thou the verses of guidance. Be engaged in the worship of thy Lord, and rise up to lead the people aright. Loose thy tongue and teach, and let thy face be bright with the fire of God's love. Rest thou not for a moment, seek thou to draw no easeful breath. Thus mayest thou become a sign and symbol of God's love, and a banner of His grace.

—'Abdu'l-Bahá

Courage

1

The source of courage and power is the promotion of the Word of God, and steadfastness in His Love.

—*Bahá'u'lláh*

2

O handmaid of God! In this wondrous dispensation* in which the Ancient Beauty† and the Manifest Light—may my spirit be sacrificed for His loved ones—hath risen from the horizon of age-old hopes, women have assumed the attributes of men in showing forth steadfastness in the Cause of God, and revealing the heroism and might of fearless men. They invaded the arena of

---

* A dispensation is the period of time during which the laws and teachings of a Prophet of God have spiritual authority. The dispensation of Bahá'u'lláh began in 1852, when He experienced the first intimation of His mission, and will last until the advent of the next Manifestation of God, which Bahá'u'lláh asserts will occur in no less than one thousand years.

† A translation of *Jamál-i-Qadím,* a name of God that is also used as a title of Bahá'u'lláh.

mystic knowledge and hoisted aloft the banner on the heights of certitude. Thou, too, must make a mighty effort and show forth supreme courage. Exert thyself and taste of the sweetness of a heavenly draught, for the sweet taste of the love of God will linger on to the end that hath no end.

—'Abdu'l-Bahá

3

In this great Cycle and wondrous Dispensation some women have been raised up who were the emblems of unity and ensigns of oneness, for the revelation of divine bestowals is received by men and women in equal measure. "Verily the most honored in the sight of God is the most virtuous amongst you"* is applicable to both men and women, to servants and handmaidens. All are under the shadow of the Word of God and all derive their strength from the bounties of the Lord. Therefore, do not consider thyself to be insignificant by doubting what a handmaiden living behind the veil† can do. . . .

---

* Qur'án 49:13.

† The Bahá'í Faith began in Persia at a time when women were expected to wear a veil or head covering in public. This refers to the limitations placed on women during that time.

With a firm heart, a steadfast step and an eloquent tongue arise to spread the Word of God and say: "O God, although I am sitting concealed behind the screen of chastity and am restricted by the veil and exigencies of modesty,* my cherished hope is to raise the banner of service and to become a maidservant at Thy Holy Threshold; to ride on a charger and penetrate the army of the ignorant, defeat the mighty regiments and subvert the foundations of error and violation. Thou art the Helper of the weak, Thou art the Sustainer of the poor, Thou art the Succorer of the handmaidens. Verily, Thou art the Almighty and All-Powerful."

—'Abdu'l-Bahá

4

Do not despair! Work steadily. Sincerity and love will conquer hate. How many seemingly impossible events are coming to pass in these days! Set your faces steadily towards the Light of the World. Show love to all; "Love is the breath of the Holy Spirit in the heart of Man." Take courage! God

---

* In Persia, a screen of cloth would separate men and women from each other at mixed gatherings. The veil was worn by women as a symbol of their modesty and chastity.

never forsakes His children who strive and work and pray! Let your hearts be filled with the strenuous desire that tranquillity and harmony may encircle all this warring world. So will success crown your efforts, and with the universal brotherhood will come the Kingdom of God in peace and goodwill.

—'Abdu'l-Bahá

5

L ove and obey your Heavenly Father, and rest assured that Divine help is yours. Verily I say unto you that you shall indeed conquer the world!

Only have faith, patience and courage—this is but the beginning, but surely you will succeed, for God is with you!

—'Abdu'l-Bahá

6

S trive as much as ye can to turn wholly toward the Kingdom, that ye may acquire innate courage and ideal power.

—'Abdu'l-Bahá

7

R est assured that the breathings of the Holy Spirit will loosen thy tongue. Speak, therefore; speak out with great courage at every meeting. When thou art about to begin thine address, turn first to Bahá'u'lláh, and ask for the confirmations of the Holy Spirit, then open thy lips and say whatever is suggested to thy heart; this, however, with the utmost courage, dignity and conviction.

—'Abdu'l-Bahá

8

It is my earnest hope that you, His distinguished leaf, together with the other maidservants of the All-Merciful in that land, may be so enkindled by the flame set ablaze by the hand of God as to illumine the whole world through the quickening energy of the love of God, and that through the eloquence of your speech, the fluency of your tongue, and the confirmations of the Holy Spirit you will be empowered to expound divine wisdom in such manner that men of eloquence, and the scholars and sages of the world, will be lost in bewilderment.

—Bahíyyih Khánum

Detachment

1

Glory to Thee, O my God! One of Thy hand-maidens, who hath believed in Thee and in Thy signs, hath entered beneath the shadow of the tree of Thy oneness. Give her to quaff, O my God, by Thy Name, the Manifest and the Hidden, of Thy choice sealed Wine that it may take her away from her own self, and make her to be entirely devoted to Thy remembrance, and wholly detached from any one beside Thee.

Now that Thou hast revealed unto her the knowledge of Thee, O my Lord, deny her not, by Thy bounty, Thy grace; and now that Thou hast called her unto Thyself, drive her not away from Thee, through Thy favor. Supply her, then, with that which excelleth all that can be found on Thine earth. Thou art, verily, the Most Bountiful, Whose grace is immense.

Wert Thou to bestow on one of Thy creatures what would equal the kingdoms of earth and heaven, it would still not diminish by even as much as an atom the immensity of Thy dominion. Far greater art Thou than the Great One men are wont to call Thee, for such a title is but one of

Thy names all of which were created by a mere indication of Thy will.

There is no God but Thee, the God of power, the God of glory, the God of knowledge and wisdom.

—*Bahá'u'lláh*

2

Turn thou unto God and say: O my Sovereign Lord! I am but a vassal of Thine, and Thou art, in truth, the King of kings. I have lifted my suppliant hands unto the heaven of Thy grace and Thy bounties. Send down, then, upon me from the clouds of Thy generosity that which will rid me of all save Thee, and draw me nigh unto Thyself. I beseech Thee, O my Lord, by Thy name, which Thou hast made the king of names and the manifestation of Thyself to all who are in heaven and on earth, to rend asunder the veils that have intervened between me and my recognition of the Dawning-Place of Thy signs and the Dayspring of Thy Revelation. Thou art, verily, the Almighty, the All-Powerful, the All-Bounteous. Deprive me not, O my Lord, of the fragrances of the Robe of Thy mercy in Thy days, and write down for me that which Thou hast written down for Thy handmaidens who have believed in Thee and in Thy signs, and have recognized Thee, and set their hearts towards the horizon of Thy Cause. Thou art truly the Lord of the worlds and of those who show mercy the Most Merciful. Assist me, then, O my God, to remember Thee amongst Thy handmaidens, and to aid Thy Cause in Thy lands. Accept, then, that which hath escaped me when the light of Thy countenance shone forth. Thou, indeed, hast power over all things. Glory be to Thee, O Thou in Whose hand is the kingdom of the heavens and of the earth.

—Bahá'u'lláh

3

O Lord! Unto Thee I repair for refuge, and toward all Thy signs I set my heart.

O Lord! Whether traveling or at home, and in my occupation or in my work, I place my whole trust in Thee.

Grant me then Thy sufficing help so as to make me independent of all things, O Thou Who art unsurpassed in Thy mercy!

Bestow upon me my portion, O Lord, as Thou pleasest, and cause me to be satisfied with whatsoever thou hast ordained for me.

Thine is the absolute authority to command.

—The Báb

4

O ye handmaids of the merciful Lord! How many queens of this world laid down their heads on a pillow of dust and disappeared. No fruit was left of them, no trace, no sign, not even their names. For them, no more granting of bestowals; for them, no more living at all. Not so the handmaids who ministered at the Threshold of God; these have shone forth like glittering stars in the skies of ancient glory, shedding their splendors across all the reaches of time. These have fulfilled their dearest hopes in the Abhá Paradise;* they have tasted the honey of reunion in the congregation of the Lord. Such souls as these profited from their existence here on earth: they plucked the fruit of life. As for the rest, "There surely came upon them a time when they were a thing not spoken of."

—'Abdu'l-Bahá

5

Depend thou upon God. Forsake thine own will and cling to His, set aside thine own desires and lay hold of His, that thou mayest become an example, holy, spiritual, and of the Kingdom, unto His handmaids.

—'Abdu'l-Bahá

---

* *The Most Glorious Paradise:* the spiritual world beyond this world.

6

O handmaid of the Lord! Speak thou no word of politics; thy task concerneth the life of the soul, for this verily leadeth to man's joy in the world of God. Except to speak well of them, make thou no mention of the earth's kings, and the worldly governments thereof. Rather, confine thine utterance to spreading the blissful tidings of the Kingdom of God, and demonstrating the influence of the Word of God, and the holiness of the Cause of God. Tell thou of abiding joy and spiritual delights, and godlike qualities, and of how the Sun of Truth hath risen above the earth's horizons: tell of the blowing of the spirit of life into the body of the world.

—'Abdu'l-Bahá

7

O handmaid of God, softly recite thou this commune to thy Lord, and say unto Him:

O God, my God! Fill up for me the cup of detachment from all things, and in the assembly of Thy splendors and bestowals, rejoice me with the wine of loving Thee. Free me from the assaults of passion and desire, break off from me the shackles of this nether world, draw me with rapture unto Thy supernal realm, and refresh me amongst the handmaids with the breathings of Thy holiness.

O Lord, brighten Thou my face with the lights of Thy bestowals, light Thou mine eyes with beholding the signs of Thine all-subduing might; delight my heart with the glory of Thy knowledge that encompasseth all things, gladden Thou my soul with Thy soul-reviving tidings of great joy, O Thou King of this world and the Kingdom above, O Thou Lord of dominion and might, that I may spread abroad Thy signs and tokens, and proclaim Thy Cause, and promote Thy Teachings, and serve Thy Law, and exalt Thy Word.

Thou art verily the Powerful, the Ever-Giving, the Able, the Omnipotent.

—*'Abdu'l-Bahá*

8

O my God! O my God! Glory be unto Thee for that Thou hast confirmed me to the confession of Thy oneness, attracted me unto the word of Thy singleness, enkindled me by the fire of Thy love, and occupied me with Thy mention and the service of Thy friends and maidservants.

O Lord, help me to be meek and lowly, and strengthen me in severing myself from all things and in holding to the hem of the garment of Thy glory, so that my heart may be filled with Thy love and leave no space for love of the world and attachment to its qualities.

O God! Sanctify me from all else save Thee, purge me from the dross of sins and transgressions, and cause me to possess a spiritual heart and conscience.

Verily, Thou art merciful and, verily, Thou art the Most Generous, Whose help is sought by all men.

—'Abdu'l-Bahá

Education and Training
of Children

1

A mong the greatest of all services that can possibly be rendered by man to Almighty God is the education and training of children, young plants of the Abhá Paradise,* so that these children, fostered by grace in the way of salvation, growing like pearls of divine bounty in the shell of education, will one day bejewel the crown of abiding glory.

It is, however, very difficult to undertake this service, even harder to succeed in it. I hope that thou wilt acquit thyself well in this most important of tasks, and successfully carry the day, and become an ensign of God's abounding grace; that these children, reared one and all in the holy Teachings, will develop natures like unto the sweet airs that blow across the gardens of the All-Glorious, and will waft their fragrance around the world.

—'Abdu'l-Bahá

---

* *The Most Glorious Paradise:* the spiritual world beyond this world.

2

Every day at first light, ye gather the . . . children together and teach them the communes and prayers. This is a most praiseworthy act, and bringeth joy to the children's hearts: that they should, at every morn, turn their faces toward the Kingdom and make mention of the Lord and praise His Name, and in the sweetest of voices, chant and recite.

These children are even as young plants, and teaching them the prayers is as letting the rain pour down upon them, that they may wax tender and fresh, and the soft breezes of the love of God may blow over them, making them to tremble with joy.

Blessedness awaiteth you, and a fair haven.

—'Abdu'l-Bahá

3

O thou handmaid of God!
Do thou establish a heavenly school and be thou a teacher in that house of learning. Educate the children in the things of God; and, even as pearls, rear them in the heart of the shell of divine guidance.

Strive thou with heart and soul; see to it that the children are raised up to embody the highest perfections of humankind, to such a degree that every one of them will be trained in the use of the mind, in acquiring knowledge, in humility and lowliness, in dignity, in ardor and love.

—'Abdu'l-Bahá

4

If the mother is educated then her children will be well taught. When the mother is wise, then will the children be led into the path of wisdom. If the mother be religious she will show her children how they should love God. If the mother is moral she guides her little ones into the ways of uprightness.

It is clear therefore that the future generation depends on the mothers of today. Is not this a vital responsibility for the woman? Does she not require every possible advantage to equip her for such a task?

Therefore, surely, God is not pleased that so important an instrument as woman should suffer from want of training in order to attain the perfections desirable and necessary for her great life's work! Divine Justice demands that the rights of both sexes should be equally respected since neither is superior to the other in the eyes of Heaven. Dignity before God depends, not on sex, but on purity and luminosity of heart. Human virtues belong equally to all!

—'Abdu'l-Bahá

5

It is incumbent upon the girls of this glorious era to be fully versed in the various branches of knowledge, in sciences and the arts and all the wonders of this pre-eminent time, that they may then educate their children and train them from their earliest days in the ways of perfection.

—'Abdu'l-Bahá

6

Education holds an important place in the new order of things. The education of each child is compulsory. If there is not money enough in a family to educate both the girl and the boy the money must be dedicated to the girl's education, for she is the potential mother. If there are no parents the community must educate the child. In addition to this widespread education each child must be taught a profession, art, or trade, so that every member of the community will be enabled to earn his own livelihood. Work done in the spirit of service is the highest form of worship.

—'Abdu'l-Bahá

7

The decision-making agencies involved would do well to consider giving first priority to the education of women and girls, since it is through educated mothers that the benefits of knowledge can be most effectively and rapidly diffused throughout society. In keeping with the requirements of the times, consideration should also be given to teaching the concept of world citizenship as part of the standard education of every child.

—Universal House of Justice

Equality

1

In this Day the Hand of divine grace hath removed all distinctions. The servants of God and His handmaidens are regarded on the same plane. Blessed is the servant who hath attained unto that which God hath decreed, and likewise the leaf moving in accordance with the breezes of His will. This favor is great and this station lofty. His bounties and bestowals are ever present and manifest. Who is able to offer befitting gratitude for His successive bestowals and continuous favors?

—*Bahá'u'lláh*

2

All should know, and in this regard attain the splendors of the sun of certitude, and be illumined thereby: Women and men have been and will always be equal in the sight of God. The Dawning-Place of the Light of God sheddeth its radiance upon all with the same effulgence. Verily God created women for men, and men for women. The most beloved of people before God are the most steadfast and those who have surpassed others in their love for God, exalted be His glory. . . .

—*Bahá'u'lláh*

3

The friends of God must be adorned with the ornament of justice, equity, kindness and love. As they do not allow themselves to be the object of cruelty and transgression, in like manner they should not allow such tyranny to visit the handmaidens of God. He, verily, speaketh the truth and commandeth that which benefitteth His servants and handmaidens. He is the Protector of all in this world and the next.

—*Bahá'u'lláh*

4

And among the teachings of Bahá'u'lláh is the equality of women and men. The world of humanity has two wings—one is women and the other men. Not until both wings are equally developed can the bird fly. Should one wing remain weak, flight is impossible. Not until the world of women becomes equal to the world of men in the acquisition of virtues and perfections, can success and prosperity be attained as they ought to be.

—*'Abdu'l-Bahá*

5

One of the potentialities hidden in the realm of humanity was the capability or capacity of womanhood. Through the effulgent rays of divine illumination the capacity of woman has become so awakened and manifest in this age that equality of man and woman is an established fact. . . .

The truth is that all mankind are the creatures and servants of one God, and in His estimate all are human. Man is a generic term applying to all humanity. The biblical statement "Let us make man in our image, after our likeness" does not mean that woman was not created. The image and likeness of God apply to her as well. . . .

To accept and observe a distinction which God has not intended in creation is ignorance and superstition. The fact which is to be considered, however, is that woman, having formerly been deprived, must now be allowed equal opportunities with man for education and training. There must be no difference in their education. Until the reality of equality between man and woman is fully established and attained, the highest social development of mankind is not possible.

—'Abdu'l-Bahá

6

For the world of humanity consists of two parts or members: one is woman; the other is man. Until these two members are equal in strength, the oneness of humanity cannot be established, and the happiness and felicity of mankind will not be a reality. God willing, this is to be so.

—*'Abdu'l-Bahá*

7

In past ages it was held that woman and man were not equal—that is to say, woman was considered inferior to man, even from the standpoint of her anatomy and creation. She was considered especially inferior in intelligence, and the idea prevailed universally that it was not allowable for her to step into the arena of important affairs. In some countries man went so far as to believe and teach that woman belonged to a sphere lower than human. But in this century, which is the century of light and the revelation of mysteries, God is proving to the satisfaction of humanity that all this is ignorance and error; nay, rather, it is well established that mankind and womankind as parts of composite humanity are coequal and that no difference in estimate is allowable, for all are human. The conditions in past centuries were due to woman's lack of opportunity. She was denied the right and privilege of education and left in her undeveloped state. Naturally, she could not and did not advance. In reality, God has created all mankind, and in the estimation of God there is no distinction as to male and female. The one whose heart is pure is acceptable in His sight, be that one man or woman. God does not inquire, "Art thou woman or art thou man?" He judges human actions. If these are acceptable in the threshold of the Glorious One, man and woman will be equally recognized and rewarded.

—'Abdu'l-Bahá

8

Woman's lack of progress and proficiency has been due to her need of equal education and opportunity. Had she been allowed this equality, there is no doubt she would be the counterpart of man in ability and capacity. The happiness of mankind will be realized when women and men coordinate and advance equally, for each is the complement and helpmeet of the other.

—'Abdu'l-Bahá

9

Women have equal rights with men upon earth; in religion and society they are a very important element. As long as women are prevented from attaining their highest possibilities, so long will men be unable to achieve the greatness which might be theirs.

—'Abdu'l-Bahá

10

According to the spirit of this age, women must advance and fulfill their mission in all departments of life, becoming equal to men. They must be on the same level as men and enjoy equal rights. This is my earnest prayer and it is one of the fundamental principles of Bahá'u'lláh.

—'Abdu'l-Bahá

11

The world of humanity has two wings, as it were: One is the female; the other is the male. If one wing be defective, the strong perfect wing will not be capable of flight. The world of humanity has two hands. If one be imperfect, the capable hand is restricted and unable to perform its duties. God is the Creator of mankind. He has endowed both sexes with perfections and intelligence, given them physical members and organs of sense, without differentiation or distinction as to superiority; therefore, why should woman be considered inferior? This is not according to the plan and justice of God. He has created them equal; in His estimate there is no question of sex. The one whose heart is purest, whose deeds are most perfect, is acceptable to God, male or female.

—'Abdu'l-Bahá

12

In this Revelation of Bahá'u'lláh, the women go neck and neck with the men. In no movement will they be left behind. Their rights with men are equal in degree. They will enter all the administrative branches of politics. They will attain in all such a degree as will be considered the very highest station of the world of humanity and will take part in all affairs. Rest ye assured. Do ye not look upon the present conditions; in the not far distant future the world of women will become all-refulgent and all-glorious, *For His Holiness Bahá'u'lláh Hath Willed It so!* At the time of elections the right to vote is the inalienable right of women, and the entrance of women into all human departments is an irrefutable and incontrovertible question. No soul can retard or prevent it.

—'Abdu'l-Bahá

13

Know thou, O handmaid, that in the sight of Bahá,* women are accounted the same as men, and God hath created all humankind in His own image, and after His own likeness. That is, men and women alike are the revealers of His

---

* Bahá'u'lláh.

names and attributes, and from the spiritual view-point there is no difference between them. Who-soever draweth nearer to God, that one is the most favored, whether man or woman. How many a handmaid, ardent and devoted, hath, within the sheltering shade of Bahá, proved superior to the men, and surpassed the famous of the earth.

—'Abdu'l-Bahá

14

Equality between men and women does not, in-deed physiologically it cannot, mean identity of functions. In some things women excel men, for others men are better fitted than women, while in very many things the difference of sex is of no effect at all. The differences of function are most apparent in family life.

—Universal House of Justice

Family

1

The beginning of magnanimity is when man expendeth his wealth on himself, on his family and on the poor among his brethren in his Faith.

—Bahá'u'lláh

2

Glory be unto Thee, O Lord my God! I beg Thee to forgive me and those who support Thy Faith. Verily, Thou art the sovereign Lord, the Forgiver, the Most Generous. O my God! Enable such servants of Thine as are deprived of knowledge to be admitted into Thy Cause; for once they learn of Thee, they bear witness to the truth of the Day of Judgment and do not dispute the revelations of Thy bounty. Send down upon them the tokens of Thy grace, and grant them, wherever they reside, a liberal share of that which Thou hast ordained for the pious among Thy servants. Thou art in truth the Supreme Ruler, the All-Bounteous, the Most Benevolent.

O my God! Let the outpourings of Thy bounty and blessings descend upon homes whose inmates have embraced Thy Faith, as a token of Thy grace and as a mark of loving-kindness from Thy presence. Verily, unsurpassed art Thou in granting forgiveness. Should Thy bounty be withheld from anyone, how could he be reckoned among the followers of the Faith in Thy Day?

Bless me, O my God, and those who will believe in Thy signs on the appointed Day, and such as cherish my love in their hearts—a love which Thou dost instill into Them. Verily, Thou art the Lord of righteousness, the Most Exalted.

—The Báb

3

According to the teachings of Bahá'u'lláh the family, being a human unit, must be educated according to the rules of sanctity. All the virtues must be taught the family. The integrity of the family bond must be constantly considered, and the rights of the individual members must not be transgressed. The rights of the son, the father, the mother —none of them must be transgressed, none of them must be arbitrary. Just as the son has certain obligations to his father, the father, likewise, has certain obligations to his son. The mother, the sister and other members of the household have their certain prerogatives. All these rights and prerogatives must be conserved, yet the unity of the family must be sustained. The injury of one shall be considered the injury of all; the comfort of each, the comfort of all; the honor of one, the honor of all.

—'Abdu'l-Bahá

4

A family is a nation in miniature. Simply enlarge the circle of the household, and you have the nation. Enlarge the circle of nations, and you have all humanity. The conditions surrounding the family surround the nation. The happenings in the family are the happenings in the life of the nation. Would it add to the progress and advancement of a family if dissensions should arise among its members, all fighting, pillaging each other, jealous and revengeful of injury, seeking selfish advantage? Nay, this would be the cause of the effacement of progress and advancement. So it is in the great family of nations, for nations are but an aggregate of families. Therefore, as strife and dissension destroy a family and prevent its progress, so nations are destroyed and advancement hindered.

—'Abdu'l-Bahá

Husbands

5

O God, my God! This Thy handmaid is calling upon Thee, trusting in Thee, turning her face unto Thee, imploring Thee to shed Thy heavenly bounties upon her, and to disclose unto her Thy spiritual mysteries, and to cast upon her the lights of Thy Godhead.

O my Lord! Make the eyes of my husband to see. Rejoice Thou his heart with the light of the knowledge of Thee, draw Thou his mind unto Thy luminous beauty, cheer Thou his spirit by revealing unto him Thy manifest splendors.

O my Lord! Lift Thou the veil from before his sight. Rain down Thy plenteous bounties upon him, intoxicate him with the wine of love for Thee, make him one of Thy angels whose feet walk upon this earth even as their souls are soaring through the high heavens. Cause him to become a brilliant lamp, shining out with the light of Thy wisdom in the midst of Thy people.

Verily Thou art the Precious, the Ever-Bestowing, the Open of Hand.

—'Abdu'l-Bahá

Infants

6

Praised be Thou, O Lord my God! Graciously grant that this infant be fed from the breast of Thy tender mercy and loving providence and be nourished with the fruit of Thy celestial trees. Suffer him not to be committed to the care of anyone save Thee, inasmuch as Thou, Thyself, through the potency of thy sovereign will and power, didst create and call him into being. There is none other God but Thee, the Almighty, the All-Knowing.

Lauded art Thou, O my Best Beloved, waft over him the sweet savors of Thy transcendent bounty and the fragrances of Thy holy bestowals. Enable him then to seek shelter beneath the shadow of Thy most exalted Name, O Thou Who holdest in Thy grasp the kingdom of names and attributes. Verily, Thou art potent to do what Thou willest, and Thou art indeed the Mighty, the Exalted, the Ever-Forgiving, the Gracious, the Generous, the Merciful.

—*Bahá'u'lláh*

7

O Thou peerless Lord! Let this suckling babe be nursed from the breast of Thy loving-kindness, guard it within the cradle of Thy safety and protection and grant that it be reared in the arms of Thy tender affection.

—'Abdu'l-Bahá

8

O God! Rear this little babe in the bosom of Thy love, and give it milk from the breast of Thy Providence. Cultivate this fresh plant in the rose garden of Thy love and aid it to grow through the showers of Thy bounty. Make it a child of the kingdom, and lead it to Thy heavenly realm. Thou art powerful and kind, and Thou art the Bestower, the Generous, the Lord of surpassing bounty.

—'Abdu'l-Bahá

Children

9

O Lord, my God! This is a child that hath sprung from the loins of one of Thy servants to whom Thou hast granted a distinguished station in the Tablets of Thine irrevocable decree in the Books of Thy behest.

I beseech Thee by Thy name, whereby everyone is enabled to attain the object of his desire, to grant that this child may become a more mature soul amongst Thy servants; cause him to shine forth through the power of Thy name, enable him to utter Thy praise, to set his face towards Thee and to draw nigh unto Thee. Verily, it is Thou Who hast, from everlasting, been powerful to do as Thou willest and Who wilt, to eternity, remain potent to do as Thou pleasest. There is none other God but Thee, the Exalted, the August, the Subduer, the Mighty, the All-Compelling.

—*Bahá'u'lláh*

10

O God! Educate these children. These children are the plants of Thine orchard, the flowers of Thy meadow, the roses of Thy garden. Let Thy rain fall upon them; let the Sun of Reality shine upon them with Thy love. Let Thy breeze refresh them in order that they may be trained, grow and develop, and appear in the utmost beauty. Thou art the Giver. Thou art the Compassionate.

—*'Abdu'l-Bahá*

11

O Thou kind Lord! These lovely children are the handiwork of the fingers of Thy might and the wondrous signs of Thy greatness. O God! Protect these children, graciously assist them to be educated and enable them to render service to the world of humanity. O God! These children are pearls, cause them to be nurtured within the shell of Thy loving-kindness.

Thou art the Bountiful, the All-Loving.

—*'Abdu'l-Bahá*

Daughters

12

O Thou most glorious Lord! Make this little maidservant of Thine blessed and happy; cause her to be cherished at the threshold of Thy oneness and let her drink deep from the cup of Thy love so that she may be filled with rapture and ecstasy and diffuse sweet-scented fragrance. Thou art the Mighty and the Powerful, and Thou art the All-Knowing, the All-Seeing.

—*'Abdu'l-Bahá*

Parents

13

O God, my God! I implore Thee by the blood of Thy true lovers who were so enraptured by Thy sweet utterance that they hastened unto the Pinnacle of Glory, the site of the most glorious martyrdom, and I beseech Thee by the mysteries which lie enshrined in Thy knowledge and by the pearls that are treasured in the ocean of Thy bounty to grant forgiveness unto me and unto my father and my mother. Of those who show forth mercy, Thou art in truth the Most Merciful. No God is there but Thee, the Ever-Forgiving, the All-Bountiful.

—*Bahá'u'lláh*

14

Say, O My people! Show honor to your parents and pay homage to them. This will cause blessings to descend upon you from the clouds of the bounty of your Lord, the Exalted, the Great.

—*Bahá'u'lláh*

15

I beg Thy forgiveness, O my God, and implore pardon after the manner Thou wishest Thy servants to direct themselves to Thee. I beg of Thee to wash away our sins as befitteth Thy Lordship, and to forgive me, my parents, and those who in Thy estimation have entered the abode of Thy love in a manner which is worthy of Thy transcendent sovereignty and well beseemeth the glory of Thy celestial power.

O my God! Thou hast inspired my soul to offer its supplication to Thee, and but for Thee, I would

not call upon Thee. Lauded and glorified art Thou;
I yield Thee praise inasmuch as Thou didst reveal
Thyself unto me, and I beg Thee to forgive me,
since I have fallen short in my duty to know Thee
and have failed to walk in the path of Thy love.

—The Báb

16

It is seemly that the servant should, after each
prayer, supplicate God to bestow mercy and forgiveness upon his parents. Thereupon God's call
will be raised: "Thousand upon thousand of what
thou hast asked for thy parents shall be thy recompense!" Blessed is he who remembereth his parents
when communing with God. There is, verily, no
God but Him, the Mighty, the Well-Beloved.

—The Báb

Forgiveness

1

All Thy servants, O my God, are occupied with their own selves, so great have been the troubles which, as decreed by Thee, have encompassed them on every side. My tongue, however, is busied in extolling Thy chosen ones, and my heart in remembering them that are dear to Thee and are wholly subject to Thy will.

Look not on my state, O my God, nor my failure to serve Thee, nay rather regard the oceans of Thy mercy and favors, and the things that beseem Thy glory and Thy forgiveness and befit Thy loving-kindness and bounties. Thou art, verily, the Ever-Forgiving, the Most Generous.

—Bahá'u'lláh

2

My God, Thou Whom I adore and worship, Who art Most Powerful! I testify that no description by any created thing can ever reveal Thee, and no praise which any being is able to utter can express Thee. Neither the comprehension of any one in the whole world, nor the intelligence of any of its peoples, can, as it befitteth Thee, gain

admittance into the court of Thy holiness, or un-
ravel Thy mystery. What sin hath kept the inmates
of the city of Thy names so far from Thine all-glorious Horizon, and deprived them of access to Thy
most great Ocean? One single letter of Thy Book is
the mother of all utterances, and a word therefrom
the begetter of all creation. What ingratitude have
Thy servants shown forth that Thou hast withheld
them, one and all, from recognizing Thee? A drop
out of the ocean of Thy mercy sufficeth to quench
the flames of hell, and a spark of the fire of Thy love
is enough to set ablaze a whole world.

O Thou Who art the All-Knowing! Wayward
though we be, we still cling to Thy bounty; and
though ignorant, we still set our faces toward the
ocean of Thy wisdom. Thou art that All-Bountiful Who art not deterred by a multitude of sins
from vouchsafing Thy bounty, and the flow of
Whose gifts is not arrested by the withdrawal of
the peoples of the world. From eternity the door
of Thy grace hath remained wide open. A dew-
drop out of the ocean of Thy mercy is able to adorn
all things with the ornament of sanctity, and a
sprinkling of the waters of Thy bounty can cause
the entire creation to attain unto true wealth.

Lift not the veil, O Thou Who art the Concealer!
From eternity the tokens of Thy bounty have encompassed the universe, and the splendors of Thy

Most Great Name have been shed over all created things. Deny not Thy servants the wonders of Thy grace. Cause them to be made aware of Thee, that they may bear witness to Thy unity, and enable them to recognize Thee, that they may hasten towards Thee. Thy mercy hath embraced the whole creation, and Thy grace hath pervaded all things. From the billows of the ocean of Thy generosity the seas of eagerness and enthusiasm were revealed. Thou art what Thou art. Aught except Thee is unworthy of any mention unless it entereth beneath Thy shadow, and gaineth admittance into Thy court.

Whatever betide us, we beseech Thine ancient forgiveness, and seek Thine all-pervasive grace. Our hope is that Thou wilt deny no one Thy grace, and wilt deprive no soul of the ornament of fairness and justice. Thou art the King of all bounty, and the Lord of all favors, and supreme over all who are in heaven and on earth.

—Bahá'u'lláh

3

Thou seest, O Lord, our suppliant hands lifted up towards the heaven of Thy favor and bounty. Grant that they may be filled with the treasures of Thy munificence and bountiful favor. Forgive us, and our fathers, and our mothers, and fulfill whatsoever we have desired from the ocean of Thy grace and Divine generosity. Accept, O Beloved of our hearts, all our works in Thy path. Thou art, verily, the Most Powerful, the Most Exalted, the Incomparable, the One, the Forgiving, the Gracious.

—Baha'u'llah

4

O God our Lord! Protect us through Thy grace from whatsoever may be repugnant unto Thee, and vouchsafe unto us that which well beseemeth Thee. Give us more out of Thy bounty, and bless us. Pardon us for the things we have done, and wash away our sins, and forgive us with Thy gracious forgiveness. Verily, Thou art the Most Exalted, the Self-Subsisting.

Thy loving providence hath encompassed all created things in the heavens and on the earth, and Thy forgiveness hath surpassed the whole creation. Thine is sovereignty; in Thy hand are the Kingdoms of Creation and Revelation; in Thy right hand Thou holdest all created things, and within Thy grasp are the assigned measures of forgiveness. Thou forgivest whomsoever among Thy servants Thou pleasest. Verily, Thou art the Ever-Forgiving, the All-Loving. Nothing whatsoever escapeth Thy knowledge, and naught is there which is hidden from Thee.

O God our Lord! Protect us through the potency of Thy might, enable us to enter Thy wondrous surging ocean, and grant us that which well befitteth Thee.

Thou art the Sovereign Ruler, the Mighty Doer, the Exalted, the All-Loving.

—The Báb

5

I beg Thee to forgive me, O my Lord, for every mention but the mention of Thee, and for every praise but the praise of Thee, and for every delight but delight in Thy nearness, and for every pleasure but the pleasure of communion with Thee, and for every joy but the joy of Thy love and of Thy good-pleasure, and for all things pertaining unto me which bear no relationship unto Thee, O Thou Who art the Lord of lords, He Who provideth the means and unlocketh the doors.

—The Báb

6

O my God! There is no one but Thee to allay the anguish of my soul, and Thou art my highest aspiration, O my God. My heart is wedded to none save Thee and such as Thou dost love. I solemnly declare that my life and death are both for Thee. Verily Thou art incomparable and hast no partner.

O my Lord! I beg Thee to forgive me for shutting myself out from Thee. By Thy glory and majesty, I have failed to befittingly recognize Thee and to worship Thee, while Thou dost make Thyself known unto me and callest me to remembrance as beseemeth Thy station. Grievous woe would betide me, O my Lord, wert Thou to take hold of me by reason of my misdeeds and trespasses. No helper do I know of other than Thee. No refuge do I have to flee to save Thee. None among Thy creatures can dare to intercede with Thyself without Thy leave. I hold fast to Thy love before Thy court, and, according to Thy bidding, I earnestly pray unto Thee as befitteth Thy glory. I beg Thee to heed my call as Thou hast promised me. Verily Thou art God; no God is there but Thee. Alone and unaided, Thou art independent of all created things. Neither can the devotion of Thy lovers profit Thee, nor the evil doings of the faithless harm Thee. Verily Thou art my God, He Who will never fail in His promise.

O my God! I beseech Thee by the evidences of Thy favor, to let me draw nigh to the sublime heights of Thy holy presence, and protect me from inclining myself toward the subtle allusions of aught else but Thee. Guide my steps, O my God, unto that which is acceptable and pleasing to Thee. Shield me, through Thy might, from the fury of Thy wrath and chastisement, and hold me back from entering habitations not desired by Thee.

—*The Báb*

7

O Thou forgiving Lord! Thou art the shelter of all these Thy servants. Thou knowest the secrets and art aware of all things. We are all helpless, and Thou art the Mighty, the Omnipotent. We are all sinners, and Thou art the Forgiver of sins, the Merciful, the Compassionate. O Lord! Look not at our shortcomings. Deal with us according to Thy grace and bounty. Our shortcomings are many, but the ocean of Thy forgiveness is boundless. Our weakness is grievous, but the evidences of Thine aid and assistance are clear. Therefore, confirm and strengthen us. Enable us to do that which is worthy of Thy holy Threshold. Illumine our hearts, grant us discerning eyes and attentive ears. Resuscitate the dead and heal the sick. Bestow wealth upon the poor and give peace and security to the fearful. Accept us in Thy kingdom and illumine us with the light of guidance. Thou art the Powerful and the Omnipotent. Thou art the Generous. Thou art the Clement. Thou art the Kind.

—'Abdu'l-Bahá

Grace

1

Suffer me, O my God, to draw nigh unto Thee, and to abide within the precincts of Thy court, for remoteness from Thee hath well-nigh consumed me. Cause me to rest under the shadow of the wings of Thy grace, for the flame of my separation from Thee hath melted my heart within me. Draw me nearer unto the river that is life indeed, for my soul burneth with thirst in its ceaseless search after Thee. My sighs, O my God, proclaim the bitterness of mine anguish, and the tears I shed attest my love for Thee.

I beseech Thee, by the praise wherewith Thou praisest Thyself and the glory wherewith Thou glorifiest Thine own Essence, to grant that we may be numbered among them that have recognized Thee and acknowledged Thy sovereignty in Thy days. Help us then to quaff, O my God, from the fingers of mercy the living waters of Thy loving-kindness, that we may utterly forget all else except Thee, and be occupied only with Thy Self. Powerful art Thou to do what Thou willest. No God is there beside Thee, the Mighty, the Help in Peril, the Self-Subsisting.

Glorified be Thy name, O Thou Who art the King of all Kings!

—*Bahá'u'lláh*

2

The hearts that yearn after Thee, O my God, are burnt up with the fire of their longing for Thee, and the eyes of them that love Thee weep sore by reason of their crushing separation from Thy court, and the voice of the lamentation of such as have set their hopes on Thee hath gone forth throughout Thy dominions.

Thou hast Thyself, O my God, protected them, by Thy sovereign might, from both extremities. But for the burning of their souls and the sighing of their hearts, they would be drowned in the midst of their tears, and but for the flood of their tears they would be burnt up by the fire of their hearts and the heat of their souls. Methinks, they are like the angels which Thou hast created of snow and of fire. Wilt Thou, despite such vehement longing, O my God, debar them from Thy presence, or drive them away, notwithstanding such fervor, from the door of Thy mercy? All hope is ready to be extinguished in the hearts of Thy chosen ones, O my God! Where are the breezes of Thy grace? They are hemmed in on all sides by their enemies;

where are the ensigns of Thy triumph which Thou didst promise in Thy Tablets?

Thy glory is my witness! At each daybreak they who love Thee wake to find the cup of woe set before their faces, because they have believed in Thee and acknowledged Thy signs. Though I firmly believe that Thou hast a greater compassion on them than they have on their own selves, though I recognize that Thou hast afflicted them for no other purpose except to proclaim Thy Cause, and to enable them to ascend into the heaven of Thine eternity and the precincts of Thy court, yet Thou knowest full well the frailty of some of them, and art aware of their impatience in their sufferings.

Help them through Thy strengthening grace, I beseech Thee, O my God, to suffer patiently in their love for Thee, and unveil to their eyes what Thou hast decreed for them behind the Tabernacle of Thine unfailing protection, so that they may rush forward to meet what is preordained for them in Thy path, and may vie in hasting after tribulation in their love towards Thee. And if not, do Thou, then, reveal the standards of Thine ascendancy, and make them to be victorious over Thine adversaries, that Thy sovereignty may be manifested unto all the dwellers of Thy realm, and the power of Thy might demonstrated amidst Thy creatures. Power-

ful art Thou to do what Thou willest. No God is
there but Thee, the Omniscient, the All-Wise.

—*Bahá'u'lláh*

3

O God, my God! I beg of Thee by the dawn-
ing of the light of Thy Beauty that hath illumined all the earth, and by the glance of Thy divine compassion's eye that considereth all things, and
by the surging sea of Thy bestowals in which all
things are immersed, and by Thy streaming clouds
of bounty raining down gifts upon the essences of
all created things, and by the splendors of Thy mercy
that existed before ever the world was—to help Thy
chosen ones to be faithful, and assist Thy loved ones
to serve at Thine exalted Threshold, and cause them
to gain the victory through the battalions of Thy
might that overpowereth all things, and reinforce
them with a great fighting host from out of the
Concourse on high.

O my Lord! They are weak souls standing at
Thy door; they are paupers in Thy courtyard, des-
perate for Thy grace, in dire need of Thy succor,
turning their faces toward the kingdom of Thy
oneness, yearning for the bounties of Thy bestowals. O my Lord! Flood Thou their minds with Thy
holy light; cleanse Thou their hearts with the grace

of Thine assistance; gladden their bosoms with the fragrance of the joys that waft from Thy Company above; make bright their eyes by beholding the signs and tokens of Thy might; cause them to be the ensigns of purity, the banners of sanctity waving high above all creatures on the summits of the earth; make Thou their words to move hearts which are even as solid rock. May they arise to serve Thee and dedicate themselves to the Kingdom of Thy divinity, and set their faces toward the realm of Thy Self-Subsistence, and spread far and wide Thy signs, and be illumined by Thy streaming lights, and unfold Thy hidden mysteries. May they guide Thy servants unto gentle waters and to the fountain of Thy mercy that welleth and leapeth in the midmost heart of the Heaven of Thy oneness. May they hoist the sail of detachment upon the Ark of Salvation, and move over the seas of Thy knowledge; may they spread wide the pinions of unity and by their aid soar upward to the Kingdom of Thy singleness to become servants whom the Supreme Concourse will applaud, whose praises the dwellers in Thine all-glorious realm will utter; may they hear the heralds of the invisible world as they raise their cry of the Most Great Glad-Tidings; may they, in their longing to meet Thee, invoke and pray unto Thee, intoning wondrous orisons at the dawn of light—O my Lord Who disposest all things—shedding their tears at morningtide and even, yearning to pass into the shadow of Thy mercy that endeth never.

Help them, O my Lord, under all conditions, support them at all times with Thine angels of holiness, they who are Thine invisible hosts, Thy heavenly battalions who bring down to defeat the massed armies of this nether world.

Verily art Thou the Mighty, the Powerful, the Strong, the All-Encompassing, the One Who hath dominion over all that is.

—*'Abdu'l-Bahá*

4

O holy Lord! O Lord of loving-kindness! We stray about Thy dwelling, longing to behold Thy beauty, and loving all Thy ways. We are hapless, lowly, and of small account. We are paupers: show us mercy, give us bounty; look not upon our failings, hide Thou our endless sins. Whatever we are, still are we Thine, and what we speak and hear is praise of Thee, and it is Thy face we seek, Thy path we follow. Thou art the Lord of loving-kindness, we are sinners and astray and far from home. Wherefore, O Cloud of Mercy, grant us some drops of rain. O Flowering Bed of grace, send forth a fragrant breeze. O Sea of all bestowals, roll towards us a great wave. O Sun of Bounty, send down a shaft of light. Grant us pity, grant us grace. By Thy beauty, we come with no provision but our sins, with no good deeds to tell of, only hopes. Unless Thy concealing veil doth cover us, and Thy protection shield and cradle us, what power have these helpless souls to rise and serve Thee, what substance have these wretched ones to make a brave display? Thou Who art the Mighty, the All-Powerful, help us, favor us; withered as we are, revive us with showers from Thy clouds of grace; lowly as we are, illumine us with bright rays from the Daystar of Thy oneness. Cast Thou these thirsty fish into the ocean of Thy mercy, guide Thou this lost caravan to the shelter of Thy singleness; to the wellspring of guidance lead Thou the ones who have wandered far astray, and grant to those who have missed the path a haven within the precincts of Thy might. Lift Thou to these parched lips the bounteous and soft-flowing waters of heaven, raise up these dead to everlasting life. Grant Thou to the blind eyes that will see. Make Thou the deaf to hear, the dumb to speak. Set Thou the dispirited ablaze, make Thou the heedless mindful, warn Thou the proud, awaken those who sleep.

Thou art the Mighty, Thou art the Bestower, Thou art the Loving. Verily Thou art the Beneficent, the Most Exalted.

—*'Abdu'l-Bahá*

5

O thou who art carried away by the love of God! The Sun of Truth hath risen above the horizon of this world and cast down its beams of guidance. Eternal grace is never interrupted, and a fruit of that everlasting grace is universal peace. Rest thou assured that in this era of the spirit, the Kingdom of Peace will raise up its tabernacle on the summits of the world, and the commandments of the Prince of Peace will so dominate the arteries and nerves of every people as to draw into His sheltering shade all the nations on earth. From springs of love and truth and unity will the true Shepherd give His sheep to drink.

—*'Abdu'l-Bahá*

The Greatness of This Day

1

O My handmaiden, O My leaf! Render thou thanks unto the Best-Beloved of the world for having attained this boundless grace at a time when the world's learned and most distinguished men have remained deprived thereof. We have designated thee "a leaf" that thou mayest, like unto leaves, be stirred by the gentle wind of the Will of God—exalted be His glory—even as the leaves of the trees are stirred by onrushing winds. Yield thou thanks unto thy Lord by virtue of this brilliant utterance. Wert thou to perceive the sweetness of the title "O My handmaiden" thou wouldst find thyself detached from all mankind, devoutly engaged day and night in communion with Him Who is the sole Desire of the world.

In words of incomparable beauty We have made fitting mention of such leaves and handmaidens as have quaffed from the living waters of heavenly grace and have kept their eyes directed towards God. Happy and blessed are they indeed. Ere long shall God reveal their station whose loftiness no word can befittingly express nor any description adequately describe.

We admonish thee to do that which will serve to promote the interests of the Cause of God amongst men and women. He doth hear the call of the friends and beholdeth their actions. Verily, He is the Hearing and the Seeing.

Upon thee and upon them be the glory of God, the Powerful, the All-Knowing, the All-Wise.

—*Bahá'u'lláh*

2

O handmaid of God! Hearken unto the Voice of the Lord of Names, Who from His Prison* hath directed His gaze towards thee and is making mention of thee.

He hath extended assistance to every wayfarer, hath graciously responded to every petitioner and granted admittance to every seeker after truth. In this Day the Straight Path is made manifest, the Balance of divine justice is set and the light of the sun of His bounty is resplendent, yet the oppressive darkness of the people of tyranny hath, even as clouds, intervened and caused a grievous ob-

---

* In 1868 Bahá'u'lláh and His family and companions were banished to 'Akká, a prison city in northern Israel. Bahá'u'lláh was incarcerated within its barracks for over two years. Bahá'u'lláh named 'Akká "the Most Great Prison."

struction between the Daystar of heavenly grace and the people of the world. Blessed is he who hath rent the intervening veils asunder and is illumined by the radiant light of divine Revelation. Consider how numerous were those who accounted themselves among the wise and the learned, yet in the Day of God were deprived of the outpourings of heavenly bounties.

O My leaf, O My handmaid! Appreciate the value of this blessing and of this tender mercy which hath encompassed thee and guided thy steps unto the Dayspring of glory.

—*Bahá'u'lláh*

3

We beseech God to aid all the leaves to attain the knowledge of the Tree and deprive them not of the ocean of His generosity. In this day no regard is paid to loftiness or lowliness, to poverty or wealth, to nobility and lineage, to weakness or might. Whosoever recognizeth the incomparable Beloved is the possessor of true wealth and occupieth a divine station. Today, in the court of the True One, the queen of the world and her like are not worth a mustard seed, because although she may speak in the name of God, invoke the Lord of creation every day in the temple of her body, and spend large sums of earthly wealth for the development of her nation, she is deprived of recognition of the Sun of His Manifestation and is barred from the True One in Whose remembrance she is engaged.

—*Bahá'u'lláh*

4

O ye beloved, and ye handmaids of the Merciful! This is the day when the Daystar of Truth rose over the horizon of life, and its glory spread, and its brightness shone out with such power that it clove the dense and high-piled clouds and mounted the skies of the world in all its splendor. Hence do ye witness a new stirring throughout all created things.

See how, in this day, the scope of sciences and arts hath widened out, and what wondrous technical advances have been made, and to what a high degree the mind's powers have increased, and what stupendous inventions have appeared.

This age is indeed as a hundred other ages: should ye gather the yield of a hundred ages, and set that against the accumulated product of our times, the yield of this one era will prove greater than that of a hundred gone before. Take ye, for an example, the sum total of all the books that were ever written in ages past, and compare that with the books and treatises that our era hath produced:

these books, written in our day alone, far and away exceed the total number of volumes that have been written down the ages. See how powerful is the influence exerted by the Daystar of the world upon the inner essence of all created things!

But alas, a thousand times alas! The eyes see it not, the ears are deaf, and the hearts and minds are oblivious of this supreme bestowal. Strive ye then, with all your hearts and souls, to awaken those who slumber, to cause the blind to see, and the dead to rise.

—'Abdu'l-Bahá

5

In this wondrous Dispensation* the favors of the Glorious Lord are vouchsafed unto the handmaidens of the Merciful. Therefore, they should, like unto men, seize the prize and excel in the field, so that it will be proven and made manifest that the penetrative influence of the Word of God in

---

* A dispensation is the period of time during which the laws and teachings of a Prophet of God have spiritual authority. The dispensation of Bahá'u'lláh began in 1852, when He experienced the first intimation of His mission, and will last until the advent of the next Manifestation of God, which Bahá'u'lláh asserts will occur in no less than one thousand years.

this new Dispensation hath caused women to be equal with men, and that in the arena of tests they will outdo others. Therefore, the true bondsmaids of the Blessed Beauty* must be revived by the spirit of detachment, and refreshed by the breezes of attraction. With hearts overflowing with the love of God, with souls gladdened by the heavenly gladtidings, and with extreme humility and lowliness, let them speak out with eloquent speech, and praise and glorify the Great Lord, for they are the manifestations of His bounty and adorned with the crown of splendor.

—'Abdu'l-Bahá

6

Praise be to God! We are living in a century of light. Praise be to God! We are upon earth in the day of divine effulgence. Praise be to God! We are alive in this time of the manifestation of divine love. Praise be to God that we live in the day of the outpouring of heavenly bounty. Praise be to God! This is a day wherein the lights and splendors have awakened progress throughout the East and the West. Many holy souls in former times longed to witness this century, lamenting night and day, yearn-

---

* A translation of *Jamál-i-Mubárak,* a title of Bahá'u'lláh.

ing to be upon the earth in this cycle; but our presence and privilege is the beneficent gift of the Lord. In His divine mercy and absolute virtue He has bestowed this upon us, even as Christ declared, "Many are called but few are chosen." Verily, God has chosen you for His love and knowledge; God has chosen you for the worthy service of unifying mankind; God has chosen you for the purpose of investigating reality and promulgating international peace; God has chosen you for the progress and development of humanity, for spreading and proclaiming true education, for the expression of love toward your fellow creatures and the removal of prejudice; God has chosen you to blend together human hearts and give light to the human world. The doors of His generosity are wide, wide open to us; but we must be attentive, alert and mindful, occupied with service to all mankind, appreciating the bestowals of God and ever conforming to His will.

—'Abdu'l-Bahá

Healing

1

Glory be to Thee, O Lord my God! I beg of Thee by Thy Name through which He Who is Thy Beauty hath been stablished upon the throne of Thy Cause, and by Thy Name through which Thou changest all things, and gatherest together all things, and callest to account all things, and rewardest all things, and preservest all things, and sustainest all things—I beg of Thee to guard this handmaiden who hath fled for refuge to Thee, and hath sought the shelter of Him in Whom Thou Thyself art manifest, and hath put her whole trust and confidence in Thee.

She is sick, O my God, and hath entered beneath the shadow of the Tree of Thy healing; afflicted, and hath fled to the City of Thy protection; diseased, and hath sought the Fountainhead of Thy favors; sorely vexed, and hath hasted to attain the Wellspring of Thy tranquillity; burdened with sin, and hath set her face toward the court of Thy forgiveness.

Attire her, by Thy sovereignty and Thy lovingkindness, O my God and my Beloved, with the raiment of Thy balm and Thy healing, and make her quaff of the cup of Thy mercy and Thy favors. Protect her, moreover, from every affliction and ailment, from all pain and sickness, and from whatsoever may be abhorrent unto Thee.

Thou, in truth, art immensely exalted above all else except Thyself. Thou art, verily, the Healer, the All-Sufficing, the Preserver, the Ever-Forgiving, the Most Merciful.

—Bahá'u'lláh

2

O Befriended Stranger! The candle of thine heart is lighted by the hand of My power, quench it not with the contrary winds of self and passion. The healer of all thine ills is remembrance of Me, forget it not. Make My love thy treasure and cherish it even as thy very sight and life.

—Bahá'u'lláh

3

O God, my God! I beg of Thee by the ocean of Thy healing, and by the splendors of the Daystar of Thy grace, and by Thy Name through which Thou didst subdue Thy servants, and by the pervasive power of Thy most exalted Word and the potency of Thy most august Pen, and by Thy mercy that hath preceded the creation of all who are in heaven and on earth, to purge me with the waters of Thy bounty from every affliction and disorder, and from all weakness and feebleness.

Thou seest, O my Lord, Thy suppliant waiting at the door of Thy bounty, and him who hath set his hopes on Thee clinging to the cord of Thy generosity. Deny him not, I beseech Thee, the things he seeketh from the ocean of Thy grace and the Daystar of Thy loving-kindness.

Powerful art Thou to do what pleaseth Thee. There is none other God save Thee, the Ever-Forgiving, the Most Generous.

—*Bahá'u'lláh*

4

Thy name is my healing, O my God, and remembrance of Thee is my remedy. Nearness to Thee is my hope, and love for Thee is my companion. Thy mercy to me is my healing and my succor in both this world and the world to come. Thou, verily, art the All-Bountiful, the All-Knowing, the All-Wise.

—*Bahá'u'lláh*

5

Praise be to Thee, O Lord my God, my Master! Thou hearest the sighing of those who, though they long to behold Thy face, are yet separated from Thee and far distant from Thy court. Thou testifiest to the lamentations which those who have recognized Thee pour forth because of their exile from Thee and their yearning to meet Thee. I beseech Thee by those hearts which contain naught except the treasures of Thy remembrance and praise, and which show forth only the testimonies of Thy greatness and the evidences of Thy might, to bestow on Thy servants who desire Thee power to approach the seat of the revelation of the splendor of Thy glory and to assist them whose hopes are set on Thee to enter into the tabernacle of Thy transcendent favor and mercy.

Naked am I, O my God! Clothe me with the robe of Thy tender mercies. I am sore athirst; give me to drink of the oceans of Thy bountiful favor. I am a stranger; draw me nearer unto the source of Thy gifts. I am sick; sprinkle upon me the healing waters of Thy grace. I am a captive; rid me of my bondage, by the power of Thy might and through the force of Thy will, that I may soar on the wings of detachment towards the loftiest summits of Thy creation. Thou, verily, doest what Thou choosest. There is no God but Thee, the Help in Peril, the All-Glorious, the Unconstrained.

—Bahá'u'lláh

6

Praised be Thou, O Lord my God! I implore Thee, by Thy Most Great Name through which Thou didst stir up Thy servants and build up Thy cities, and by Thy most excellent titles, and Thy most august attributes, to assist Thy people to turn in the direction of Thy manifold bounties, and set their faces towards the Tabernacle of Thy wisdom. Heal Thou the sicknesses that have assailed the souls on every side, and have deterred them from directing their gaze towards the Paradise that lieth in the shelter of Thy shadowing Name, which Thou didst ordain to be the King of all names unto all who are in heaven and all who are on earth. Potent art Thou to do as pleaseth Thee. In Thy hands is the empire of all names. There is none other God but Thee, the Mighty, the Wise.

I am but a poor creature, O my Lord; I have clung to the hem of Thy riches. I am sore sick; I have held fast the cord of Thy healing. Deliver me from the ills that have encircled me, and wash me thoroughly with the waters of Thy graciousness and mercy, and attire me with the raiment of wholesomeness, through Thy forgiveness and bounty. Fix, then, mine eyes upon Thee, and rid me of all attachment to aught else except Thyself. Aid me to do what Thou desirest, and to fulfill what Thou pleasest.

Thou art truly the Lord of this life and of the next. Thou art, in truth, the Ever-Forgiving, the Most Merciful.

—*Bahá'u'lláh*

7

O handmaid of God! The prayers which were revealed to ask for healing apply both to physical and spiritual healing. Recite them, then, to heal both the soul and the body. If healing is right for the patient, it will certainly be granted; but for some ailing persons, healing would only be the cause of other ills, and therefore wisdom doth not permit an affirmative answer to the prayer.

O handmaid of God! The power of the Holy Spirit healeth both physical and spiritual ailments.

—*'Abdu'l-Bahá*

8

O thou who art turning thy face towards God! Close thine eyes to all things else, and open them to the realm of the All-Glorious. Ask whatsoever thou wishest of Him alone; seek whatsoever thou seekest from Him alone. With a look He granteth a hundred thousand hopes, with a glance He healeth a hundred thousand incurable ills, with a nod He layeth balm on every wound, with a glimpse He freeth the hearts from the shackles of grief. He doeth as He doeth, and what recourse have we? He carrieth out His Will, He ordaineth what He pleaseth. Then better for thee to bow down thy head in submission, and put thy trust in the All-Merciful Lord.

—'Abdu'l-Bahá

9

There are two ways of healing sickness, material means and spiritual means. The first is by the treatment of physicians; the second consisteth in prayers offered by the spiritual ones to God and in turning to Him. Both means should be used and practiced.

Illnesses which occur by reason of physical causes should be treated by doctors with medical remedies; those which are due to spiritual causes disappear through spiritual means. Thus an illness caused by affliction, fear, nervous impressions, will be healed more effectively by spiritual rather than by physical treatment. Hence, both kinds of treatment should be followed; they are not contradictory. Therefore thou shouldst also accept physical remedies inasmuch as these too have come from the mercy and favor of God, Who hath revealed and made manifest medical science so that His servants may profit from this kind of treatment also. Thou shouldst give equal attention to spiritual treatments, for they produce marvelous effects.

Now, if thou wishest to know the true remedy which will heal man from all sickness and will give him the health of the divine kingdom, know that it is the precepts and teachings of God. Focus thine attention upon them.

—*'Abdu'l-Bahá*

Loss of a Loved One

1

Glory be to Thee, O Lord my God! Abase not him whom Thou hast exalted through the power of Thine everlasting sovereignty, and remove not far from Thee him whom Thou hast caused to enter the tabernacle of Thine eternity. Wilt Thou cast away, O my God, him whom thou hast overshadowed with Thy Lordship, and wilt Thou turn away from Thee, O my Desire, him to whom Thou hast been a refuge? Canst Thou degrade him whom Thou hast uplifted, or forget him whom Thou didst enable to remember Thee?

Glorified, immensely glorified art Thou! Thou art He Who from everlasting hath been the King of the entire creation and its Prime Mover, and Thou wilt to everlasting remain the Lord of all created things and their Ordainer. Glorified art Thou, O my God! If Thou ceasest to be merciful unto Thy servants, who, then, will show mercy unto them; and if Thou refusest to succor thy loved ones, who is there that can succor them?

Glorified, immeasurably glorified art Thou! Thou art adored in Thy truth, and Thee do we all, verily, worship; and Thou art manifest in Thy justice, and to Thee do we all, verily, bear witness. Thou art, in truth, beloved in Thy grace. No God is there but Thee, the Help in Peril, the Self-Subsisting.

—*Bahá'u'lláh*

2

O my God! O Thou forgiver of sins, bestower of gifts, dispeller of afflictions!

Verily, I beseech Thee to forgive the sins of such as have abandoned the physical garment and have ascended to the spiritual world.

O my Lord! Purify them from trespasses, dispel their sorrows, and change their darkness into light. Cause them to enter the garden of happiness, cleanse them with the most pure water, and grant them to behold Thy splendors on the loftiest mount.

—*'Abdu'l-Bahá*

3

O my God! O my God! Verily, Thy servant, humble before the majesty of Thy divine supremacy, lowly at the door of Thy oneness, hath believed in Thee and in Thy verses, hath testified to Thy word, hath been enkindled with the fire of Thy love, hath been immersed in the depths of the ocean of Thy knowledge, hath been attracted by Thy breezes, hath relied upon Thee, hath offered his supplications to Thee, and hath been assured of Thy pardon and forgiveness. He hath abandoned this mortal life and hath flown to the kingdom of immortality, yearning for the favor of meeting Thee.

O Lord, glorify his station, shelter him under the pavilion of Thy supreme mercy, cause him to enter Thy glorious paradise, and perpetuate his existence in Thine exalted rose garden, that he may plunge into the sea of light in the world of mysteries.

Verily, Thou art the Generous, the Powerful, the Forgiver and the Bestower.

—'Abdu'l-Bahá

Loss of a Husband

4

O thou assured soul, thou maidservant of God . . . ! Be not grieved at the death of thy respected husband. He hath, verily, attained the meeting of his Lord at the seat of Truth in the presence of the potent King. Do not suppose that thou hast lost him. The veil shall be lifted and thou shalt behold his face illumined in the Supreme Concourse. Just as God, the Exalted, hath said, "Him will We surely quicken to a happy life." Supreme importance should be attached, therefore, not to this first creation but rather to the future life.

—'Abdu'l-Bahá

Loss of a Son

5

O thou beloved maidservant of God, although the loss of a son is indeed heartbreaking and beyond the limits of human endurance, yet one who knoweth and understandeth is assured that the son hath not been lost but, rather, hath stepped from this world into another, and she will find him in the divine realm. That reunion shall be for eternity, while in this world separation is inevitable and bringeth with it a burning grief.

Praise be unto God that thou hast faith, art turning thy face toward the everlasting Kingdom and believest in the existence of a heavenly world. Therefore be thou not disconsolate, do not languish, do not sigh, neither wail nor weep; for agitation and mourning deeply affect his soul in the divine realm.

That beloved child addresseth thee from the hidden world: "O thou kind Mother, thank divine Providence that I have been freed from a small and gloomy cage and, like the birds of the meadows, have soared to the divine world—a world which is spacious, illumined, and ever gay and jubilant. Therefore, lament not, O Mother, and be not grieved; I am not of the lost, nor have I been obliterated and destroyed. I have shaken off the mortal form and have raised my banner in this spiritual world. Following this separation is everlasting companionship. Thou shalt find me in the heaven of the Lord, immersed in an ocean of light."

—'Abdu'l-Bahá

Loss of a Female Relative or Friend

6

O my God, O Forgiver of sins and Dispeller of afflictions! O Thou Who art the Pardoner, the Merciful! I raise my suppliant hands to Thee, tearfully beseeching the court of Thy divine Essence to forgive, through Thy grace and clemency, Thy handmaiden who hath ascended unto the seat of truth. Cause her, O Lord, to be overshadowed by the clouds of Thy bounty and favor, immerse her in the ocean of Thy forgiveness and pardon, and enable her to enter that sanctified abode, Thy heavenly Paradise.

Thou art, verily, the Mighty, the Compassionate, the Generous, the Merciful.

—'Abdu'l-Bahá

7

O Lord, O Thou Whose mercy hath encompassed all, Whose forgiveness is transcendent, Whose bounty is sublime, Whose pardon and generosity are all-embracing, and the lights of Whose forgiveness are diffused throughout the world! O Lord of glory! I entreat Thee, fervently and tearfully, to cast upon Thy handmaiden who hath ascended unto Thee the glances of the eye of Thy mercy. Robe her in the mantle of Thy grace, bright with the ornaments of the celestial Paradise, and, sheltering her beneath the tree of Thy oneness, illumine her face with the lights of Thy mercy and compassion.

Bestow upon Thy heavenly handmaiden, O God, the holy fragrances born of the spirit of Thy forgiveness. Cause her to dwell in a blissful abode, heal her griefs with the balm of Thy reunion, and, in accordance with Thy will, grant her admission to Thy holy Paradise. Let the angels of Thy loving-kindness descend successively upon her, and shelter her beneath Thy blessed Tree. Thou art, verily, the Ever-Forgiving, the Most Generous, the All-Bountiful.

—'Abdu'l-Bahá

8

O Thou Kind Lord! This dearly cherished maidservant was attracted to Thee, and through reflection and discernment longed to attain Thy presence and enter Thy realms. With tearful eyes she fixed her gaze on the Kingdom of

Mysteries. Many a night she spent in deep communion with Thee, and many a day she lived in intimate remembrance of Thee. At every morn she was mindful of Thee, and at every eve she centered her thoughts upon Thee. Like unto a singing nightingale she chanted Thy sacred verses, and like unto a mirror she sought to reflect Thy light.

O Thou Forgiver of sins! Open Thou the way for this awakened soul to enter Thy Kingdom, and enable this bird, trained by Thy hand, to soar in the eternal rose garden. She is afire with longing to draw nigh unto Thee; enable her to attain Thy presence. She is distraught and distressed in separation from Thee; cause her to be admitted into Thy Heavenly Mansion.

O Lord! We are sinners, but Thou art the Forgiver. We are submerged in the ocean of shortcomings, but Thou art the Pardoner, the Kind. Forgive our sins and bless us with Thine abundant grace. Grant us the privilege of beholding Thy Countenance, and give us the chalice of joy and bliss. We are captives of our own transgressions, and Thou art the King of bountiful favors. We are drowned in a sea of iniquities, and Thou art the Lord of infinite mercy. Thou art the Giver, the Glorious, the Eternal, the Bounteous; and Thou art the All-Gracious, the All-Merciful, the Omnipotent, He Who is the

Bestower of gifts and the Forgiver of sins. Verily, Thou art He to Whom we turn for the remission of our failings, He Who is the Lord of lords.

—*'Abdu'l-Bahá*

Love

1

O My servants! Deprive not yourselves of the unfading and resplendent Light that shineth within the Lamp of Divine glory. Let the flame of the love of God burn brightly within your radiant hearts. Feed it with the oil of Divine guidance, and protect it within the shelter of your constancy. Guard it within the globe of trust and detachment from all else but God, so that the evil whisperings of the ungodly may not extinguish its light. O My servants! My holy, My divinely ordained Revelation may be likened unto an ocean in whose depths are concealed innumerable pearls of great price, of surpassing luster. . . . O My servants! The one true God is My witness! This most great, this fathomless and surging Ocean is near, astonishingly near, unto you. Behold it is closer to you than your life-vein! Swift as the twinkling of an eye ye can, if ye but wish it, reach and partake of this imperishable favor, this God-given grace, this incorruptible gift, this most potent and unspeakably glorious bounty.

—*Bahá'u'lláh*

2

I pray Thee, O Thou Who causest the dawn to appear, by Thy Name through Which Thou hast subjected the winds, and sent down Thy Tablets, that Thou wilt grant that we may draw near unto what Thou didst destine for us by Thy favor and bounty, and to be far removed from whatsoever may be repugnant unto Thee. Give us, then, to drink from the hands of Thy grace every day and every moment of our lives of the waters that are life indeed, O Thou Who art the Most Merciful! Make us, then, to be of them who helped Thee when fallen into the hands of those Thine enemies who are numbered with the rebellious among Thy creatures and the wicked amidst Thy people. Write down, then, for us the recompense ordained for him that hath attained Thy presence, and gazed on Thy beauty, and supply us with every good thing ordained in Thy Book for such of Thy creatures as enjoy near access to Thee.

Brighten our hearts, O my Lord, with the splendor of Thy knowledge, and illumine our sight with the light of such eyes as are fixed upon the horizon of Thy grace and the Dayspring of Thy glory. Preserve us, then, by Thy Most Great Name, Which Thou didst cause to overshadow such nations as lay claim to what Thou hast forbidden in Thy Book. This, verily, is what Thou didst announce unto us in Thy Scriptures and Thy Tablets.

Cause us, then, to be so steadfast in our love towards Thee that we will turn to none except Thee, and will be reckoned amongst them that are brought nigh to Thee, and acknowledge Thee as One Who is exalted above every comparison and is holy beyond all likeness, and will lift up our voices amongst Thy servants and cry aloud that He is the one God, the Incomparable, the Ever-Abiding, the Most Powerful, the All-Glorious, the All-Wise.

Strengthen Thou, O my Lord, the hearts of them that love Thee, that they may not be affrighted by the hosts of the infidels that are turned back from Thee, but may follow Thee in whatsoever hath been revealed by Thee. Aid them, moreover, to remember and to praise Thee, and to teach Thy Cause with eloquence and wisdom. Thou art He Who hath called Himself the Most Merciful. Ordain, then, O my God, for me and for whosoever hath sought Thee what beseemeth the excellence of Thy glory and the greatness of Thy majesty. No God is there but Thee, the Ever-Forgiving, the Most Compassionate.

—*Bahá'u'lláh*

3

Praise be to Thee, O Lord my God! I implore Thee, by Thy Name which none hath befittingly recognized, and whose import no soul hath fathomed; I beseech Thee, by Him Who is the Fountain-Head of Thy Revelation and the Dayspring of Thy signs, to make my heart to be a receptacle of Thy love and of remembrance of Thee. Knit it, then, to Thy most great Ocean, that from it may flow out the living waters of Thy wisdom and the crystal streams of Thy glorification and praise.

The limbs of my body testify to Thy unity, and the hair of my head declareth the power of Thy sovereignty and might. I have stood at the door of Thy grace with utter self-effacement and complete abnegation, and clung to the hem of Thy bounty, and fixed mine eyes upon the horizon of Thy gifts.

Do Thou destine for me, O my God, what becometh the greatness of Thy majesty, and assist me, by Thy strengthening grace, so to teach Thy Cause that the dead may speed out of their sepulchers, and rush forth towards Thee, trusting wholly in Thee, and fixing their gaze upon the orient of Thy Cause, and the dawning-place of Thy Revelation.

Thou, verily, art the Most Powerful, the Most High, the All-Knowing, the All-Wise.

—Bahá'u'lláh

4

Rain down . . . upon us, O my God, that which beseemeth Thy grace and befitteth Thy bounty. Enable us, then, O my God, to live in remembrance of Thee and to die in love of Thee, and supply us with the gift of Thy presence in Thy worlds hereafter—worlds which are inscrutable to all except Thee. Thou art our Lord and the Lord of all worlds, and the God of all that are in heaven and all that are on earth.

—*Bahá'u'lláh*

5

Love Me, that I may love thee. If thou lovest Me not, My love can in no wise reach thee. Know this, O servant.

—*Bahá'u'lláh*

6

Know thou of a certainty that Love is the secret of God's holy Dispensation,* the manifesta-

---

* A dispensation is the period of time during which the laws and teachings of a Prophet of God have spiritual authority. The dispensation of Bahá'u'lláh began in 1852, when He experienced the first intimation of His mission, and will last until the advent of the next Manifestation of God, which Bahá'u'lláh asserts will occur in no less than one thousand years.

tion of the All-Merciful, the fountain of spiritual outpourings. Love is heaven's kindly light, the Holy Spirit's eternal breath that vivifieth the human soul. Love is the cause of God's revelation unto man, the vital bond inherent, in accordance with the divine creation, in the realities of things. Love is the one means that ensureth true felicity both in this world and the next. Love is the light that guideth in darkness, the living link that uniteth God with man, that assureth the progress of every illumined soul. Love is the most great law that ruleth this mighty and heavenly cycle, the unique power that bindeth together the divers elements of this material world, the supreme magnetic force that directeth the movements of the spheres in the celestial realms. Love revealeth with unfailing and limitless power the mysteries latent in the universe. Love is the spirit of life unto the adorned body of mankind, the establisher of true civilization in this mortal world, and the shedder of imperishable glory upon every high-aiming race and nation.

—'Abdu'l-Bahá

7

Be ye the helpers of every victim of oppression, the patrons of the disadvantaged. Think ye at all times of rendering some service to every member of the human race. Pay ye no heed to aversion and rejection, to disdain, hostility, injustice: act ye in the opposite way. Be ye sincerely kind, not in appearance only. Let each one of God's loved ones center his attention on this: to be the Lord's mercy to man; to be the Lord's grace. Let him do some good to every person whose path he crosseth, and be of some benefit to him. Let him improve the character of each and all, and reorient the minds of men. In this way, the light of divine guidance will shine forth, and the blessings of God will cradle all mankind: for love is light, no matter in what abode it dwelleth; and hate is darkness, no matter where it may make its nest. O friends of God! That the hidden Mystery may stand revealed, and the secret essence of all things may be disclosed, strive ye to banish that darkness for ever and ever.

—'Abdu'l-Bahá

8

It is my hope that . . . day by day ye will love God in ever greater measure, and become more tightly bound to the Beauty that abideth forever, to Him Who is the Light of the world. For love of God and spiritual attraction do cleanse and purify the human heart and dress and adorn it with the spotless garment of holiness; and once the heart is entirely attached to the Lord, and bound over to the Blessed Perfection,* then will the grace of God be revealed.

This love is not of the body but completely of the soul. And those souls whose inner being is lit by the love of God are even as spreading rays of light, and they shine out like stars of holiness in a pure and crystalline sky. For true love, real love, is the love for God, and this is sanctified beyond the notions and imaginings of men.

Let God's beloved, each and every one, be the essence of purity, the very life of holiness, so that in every country they may become famed for their sanctity, independence of spirit, and meekness. Let them be cheered by drafts from the eternal cup of love for God, and make merry as they drink from the wine-vaults of Heaven. Let them behold the Blessed Beauty, and feel the flame and rapture of that meeting, and be struck dumb with awe and wonder. This is the station of the sincere; this is the way of the loyal; this is the brightness that shineth on the faces of those nigh unto God.

—'Abdu'l-Bahá

---

* A title of Bahá'u'lláh.

Marriage

1

Glory be unto Thee, O my God! Verily, this Thy servant and this Thy maidservant have gathered under the shadow of Thy mercy and they are united through Thy favor and generosity. O Lord! Assist them in this Thy world and Thy kingdom and destine for them every good through Thy bounty and grace. O Lord! Confirm them in Thy servitude and assist them in Thy service. Suffer them to become the signs of Thy Name in Thy world and protect them through Thy bestowals which are inexhaustible in this world and the world to come. O Lord! They are supplicating the kingdom of Thy mercifulness and invoking the realm of Thy singleness. Verily, they are married in obedience to Thy command. Cause them to become the signs of harmony and unity until the end of time. Verily, Thou art the Omnipotent, the Omnipresent and the Almighty!

—'Abdu'l-Bahá

2

O my Lord, O my Lord! These two bright orbs are wedded in Thy love, conjoined in servitude to Thy Holy Threshold, united in ministering to Thy Cause. Make Thou this marriage to be as threading lights of Thine abounding grace, O my Lord, the All-Merciful, and luminous rays of Thy bestowals, O Thou the Beneficent, the Ever-Giving, that there may branch out from this great tree boughs that will grow green and flourishing through the gifts that rain down from Thy clouds of grace.

Verily, Thou art the Generous. Verily, Thou art the Almighty. Verily, Thou art the Compassionate, the All-Merciful.

—*'Abdu'l-Bahá*

3

O ye two believers in God! The Lord, peerless is He, hath made woman and man to abide with each other in the closest companionship, and to be even as a single soul. They are two helpmates, two intimate friends, who should be concerned about the welfare of each other.

If they live thus, they will pass through this world with perfect contentment, bliss, and peace of heart, and become the object of divine grace and favor in the Kingdom of heaven. But if they do other than this, they will live out their lives in great bitterness, longing at every moment for death, and will be shamefaced in the heavenly realm.

Strive, then, to abide, heart and soul, with each other as two doves in the nest, for this is to be blessed in both worlds.

—'Abdu'l-Bahá

4

Marriage must be a union of the body and of the spirit as well, for here both husband and wife are aglow with the same wine, both are enamored of the same matchless Face, both live and move through the same spirit, both are illumined by the same glory. This connection between them is a spiritual one, hence it is a bond that will abide forever. Likewise do they enjoy strong and lasting ties in the physical world as well, for if the marriage is based both on the spirit and the body, that union is a true one, hence it will endure. If, however, the bond is physical and nothing more, it is sure to be only temporary, and must inexorably end in separation.

When, therefore, the people . . . undertake to marry, the union must be a true relationship, a spiritual coming together as well as a physical one, so that throughout every phase of life, and in all the worlds of God, their union will endure; for this real oneness is a gleaming out of the love of God.

—'Abdu'l-Bahá

5

From separation doth every kind of hurt and harm proceed, but the union of created things doth ever yield most laudable results. From the pairing of even the smallest particles in the world of being are the grace and bounty of God made manifest; and the higher the degree, the more momentous is the union. "Glory be to Him Who hath created all the pairs, of such things as earth produceth, and out of men themselves, and of things beyond their ken."* And above all other unions is that between human beings, especially when it cometh to pass in the love of God. Thus is the primal oneness made to appear; thus is laid the foundation of love in the spirit. It is certain that such a marriage as yours will cause the bestowals of God to be revealed. Wherefore do we offer you felicitations and call down blessings upon you and beg of the Blessed Beauty,† through His aid and favor, to make that wedding feast a joy to all and adorn it with the harmony of Heaven.

—'Abdu'l-Bahá

---

* Qur'án 36:36, and cf. 51:49.
† A translation of *Jamál-i-Mubárak,* a title of Bahá'u'lláh.

6

Marriage is the commitment of the two parties one to the other, and their mutual attachment of mind and heart. Each must, however, exercise the utmost care to become thoroughly acquainted with the character of the other, that the binding covenant between them may be a tie that will endure forever. Their purpose must be this: to become loving companions and comrades and at one with each other for time and eternity. . . .

The true marriage . . . is this, that husband and wife should be united both physically and spiritually, that they may ever improve the spiritual life of each other, and may enjoy everlasting unity throughout all the worlds of God.

—'Abdu'l-Bahá

Mercy

1

What outpouring flood can compare with the stream of His all-embracing grace, and what blessing can excel the evidences of so great and pervasive a mercy? There can be no doubt whatever that if for one moment the tide of His mercy and grace were to be withheld from the world, it would completely perish. For this reason, from the beginning that hath no beginning the portals of Divine mercy have been flung open to the face of all created things, and the clouds of Truth will continue to the end that hath no end to rain on the soil of human capacity, reality and personality their favors and bounties. Such hath been God's method continued from everlasting to everlasting.

—*Bahá'u'lláh*

2

This is the Day whereon the Ocean of God's mercy hath been manifested . . . the Day in which the Daystar of His loving-kindness hath shed its radiance upon them, the Day in which the clouds of His bountiful favor have overshadowed the whole of mankind. Now is the time to cheer and refresh the down-cast through the invigorating breeze of love and fellowship, and the living waters of friendliness and charity.

—*Bahá'u'lláh*

3

Magnified be Thy name, O Lord my God! Behold Thou mine eye expectant to gaze on the wonders of Thy mercy, and mine ear longing to hearken unto Thy sweet melodies, and my heart yearning for the living waters of Thy knowledge. Thou seest Thy handmaiden, O my God, standing before the habitation of Thy mercy, and calling upon Thee by Thy name which Thou hast chosen above all other names and set up over all that are in heaven and on earth. Send down upon her the breaths of Thy mercy, that she may be carried away wholly from herself, and be drawn entirely towards the seat which, resplendent with the glory of Thy face, sheddeth afar the radiance of Thy sovereignty, and is established as Thy throne. Potent art Thou to do what Thou willest. No God is there beside Thee, the All-Glorious, the Most Bountiful.

Cast not out, I entreat Thee, O my Lord, them that have sought Thee, and turn not away such as have directed their steps towards Thee, and deprive not of Thy grace all that love Thee. Thou art He, O my Lord, Who hath called Himself the God of Mercy, the Most Compassionate. Have mercy, then, upon Thy handmaiden who hath sought Thy shelter, and set her face towards Thee.

Thou art, verily, the Ever-Forgiving, the Most Merciful.

—Bahá'u'lláh

4

Unto Thee be praise, O Lord my God! I entreat Thee, by Thy signs that have encompassed the entire creation, and by the light of Thy countenance that hath illuminated all that are in heaven and on earth, and by Thy mercy that hath surpassed all created things, and by Thy grace that hath suffused the whole universe, to rend asunder the veils that shut me out from Thee, that I may hasten unto the Fountain-Head of Thy mighty inspiration, and to the Day-Spring of Thy Revelation and bountiful favors, and may be immersed beneath the ocean of Thy nearness and pleasure.

Suffer me not, O my Lord, to be deprived of the knowledge of Thee in Thy days, and divest me not of the robe of Thy guidance. Give me to drink of the river that is life indeed, whose waters have streamed forth from the Paradise (Riḍván) in which the throne of Thy Name, the All-Merciful, was established, that mine eyes may be opened, and my face be illumined, and my heart be assured, and my soul be enlightened, and my steps be made firm.

Thou art He Who from everlasting was, through the potency of His might, supreme over all things, and, through the operation of His will, was able to ordain all things. Nothing whatsoever, whether in Thy heaven or on Thy earth, can frustrate Thy purpose. Have mercy, then, upon me, O my Lord, through Thy gracious providence and generosity, and incline mine ear to the sweet melodies of the birds that warble their praise of Thee, amidst the branches of the tree of Thy oneness.

Thou art the Great Giver, the Ever-Forgiving, the Most Compassionate.

—*Bahá'u'lláh*

5

O Thou Whose face is the object of the adoration of all that yearn after Thee, Whose presence is the hope of such as are wholly devoted to Thy will, Whose nearness is the desire of all that have drawn nigh unto Thy court, Whose countenance is the companion of those who have recognized Thy truth, Whose name is the mover of the souls that long to behold Thy face, Whose voice is the true life of Thy lovers, the words of Whose mouth are as the waters of life unto all who are in heaven and on earth!

I beseech Thee, by the wrong Thou hast suffered and the ills inflicted upon Thee by the hosts of wrongful doers, to send down upon me from the clouds of Thy mercy that which will purify me of all that is not of Thee, that I may be worthy to praise Thee and fit to love Thee.

Withhold not from me, O my Lord, the things Thou didst ordain for such of Thy handmaidens as circle around Thee, and on whom are poured continually the splendors of the sun of Thy beauty and the beams of the brightness of Thy face. Thou art He Who from everlasting hath succored whosoever hath sought Thee, and bountifully favored him who hath asked Thee.

No God is there beside Thee, the Mighty, the Ever-Abiding, the All-Bounteous, the Most Generous.

—*Bahá'u'lláh*

6

O God, my God! Have mercy then upon my helpless state, my poverty, my misery, my abasement! Give me to drink from the generous cup of Thy grace and forgiveness, stir me with the sweet scents of Thy love, gladden my bosom with the light of Thy knowledge, purify my soul with the mysteries of Thy oneness, raise me to life with the gentle breeze that cometh from the gardens of Thy mercy—till I sever myself from all else but Thee, and lay hold of the hem of Thy garment of grandeur, and consign to oblivion all that is not Thee, and be companioned by the sweet breathings that waft during these Thy days, and attain unto faithfulness at Thy Threshold of Holiness, and arise to serve Thy Cause, and to be humble before Thy loved ones, and, in the presence of Thy favored ones, to be nothingness itself.

Verily art Thou the Helper, the Sustainer, the Exalted, the Most Generous.

—'Abdu'l-Bahá

7

All creatures that exist are dependent upon the Divine Bounty. Divine Mercy gives life itself. As the light of the sun shines on the whole world, so the Mercy of the infinite God is shed on all creatures. As the sun ripens the fruits of the earth, and gives life and warmth to all living beings, so shines the Sun of Truth on all souls, filling them with the fire of Divine love and understanding.

—'Abdu'l-Bahá

8

Remember not your own limitations; the help of God will come to you. Forget yourself. God's help will surely come!

When you call on the Mercy of God waiting to reinforce you, your strength will be tenfold.

—'Abdu'l-Bahá

Morning

1

I have risen this morning by Thy grace, O my God, and left my home trusting wholly in Thee, and committing myself to Thy care. Send down, then, upon me, out of the heaven of Thy mercy, a blessing from Thy side, and enable me to return home in safety even as Thou didst enable me to set out under Thy protection with my thoughts fixed steadfastly upon Thee.

There is none other God but Thee, the One, the Incomparable, the All-Knowing, the All-Wise.

—*Bahá'u'lláh*

2

I have wakened in Thy shelter, O my God, and it becometh him that seeketh that shelter to abide within the Sanctuary of Thy protection and the Stronghold of Thy defense. Illumine my inner being, O my Lord, with the splendors of the Dayspring of Thy Revelation, even as Thou didst illumine my outer being with the morning light of Thy favor.

—*Bahá'u'lláh*

3

L et each morn be better than its eve and each morrow richer than its yesterday.

—*Bahá'u'lláh*

4

O ye . . . handmaids of the Merciful! It is early morning, and the reviving winds of the Abhá Paradise* are blowing over all creation, but they can stir only the pure of heart, and only the pure sense can detect their fragrance. Only the perceiving eye beholdeth the rays of the sun; only the listening ear can hear the singing of the Concourse on high. Although the plentiful rains of spring, the bestowals of Heaven, pour down upon all things, they can only fructify good soil; they love not brackish ground, where no results of all the bounty can be shown.

Today the soft and holy breathings of the Abhá Realm† are passing over every land, but only the pure in heart draw nigh and derive a benefit therefrom. It is the hope of this wronged soul that from

---

* *The Most Glorious Paradise:* the spiritual world beyond this world.

† Another name for the Abhá Kingdom, the spiritual world beyond this world.

the grace of the Self-Subsistent One and by the manifest power of the Word of God, the heads of the unmindful may be cleared, that they may perceive these sweet savors which blow from secret rosebeds of the spirit.

—'Abdu'l-Bahá

5

Every day, in the morning when arising you should compare today with yesterday and see in what condition you are. If you see your belief is stronger and your heart more occupied with God and your love increased and your freedom from the world greater then thank God and ask for the increase of these qualities. You must begin to pray and repent for all that you have done which is wrong and you must implore and ask for help and assistance that you may become better than yesterday so that you may continue to make progress.

—'Abdu'l-Bahá

Mothers

1

Let the mothers consider that whatever concerneth the education of children is of the first importance. Let them put forth every effort in this regard, for when the bough is green and tender it will grow in whatever way ye train it. Therefore is it incumbent upon the mothers to rear their little ones even as a gardener tendeth his young plants. Let them strive by day and by night to establish within their children faith and certitude, the fear of God, the love of the Beloved of the worlds, and all good qualities and traits. Whensoever a mother seeth that her child hath done well, let her praise and applaud him and cheer his heart; and if the slightest undesirable trait should manifest itself, let her counsel the child and punish him, and use means based on reason, even a slight verbal chastisement should this be necessary. It is not, however, permissible to strike a child, or vilify him, for the child's character will be totally perverted if he be subjected to blows or verbal abuse.

—'Abdu'l-Bahá

2

O handmaids of the Merciful! Render ye thanks unto the Ancient Beauty* that ye have been raised up and gathered together in this mightiest of centuries, this most illumined of ages. As befitting thanks for such a bounty, stand ye staunch and strong in the Covenant† and, following the precepts of God and the holy Law, suckle your children from their infancy with the milk of a universal education, and rear them so that from their earliest days, within their inmost heart, their very nature, a way of life will be firmly established that will conform to the divine Teachings in all things.

For mothers are the first educators, the first mentors; and truly it is the mothers who determine the happiness, the future greatness, the courteous ways and learning and judgment, the understanding and the faith of their little ones.

—*'Abdu'l-Bahá*

3

O handmaid of God! . . . To the mothers must be given the divine Teachings and effective

---

* A translation of *Jamál-i-Qadím,* a name of God that is also used as a title of Bahá'u'lláh.

† The binding agreement between God and humanity that God will provide guidance to humankind and that humankind will accept it.

counsel, and they must be encouraged and made eager to train their children, for the mother is the first educator of the child. It is she who must, at the very beginning, suckle the newborn at the breast of God's Faith and God's Law, that divine love may enter into him even with his mother's milk, and be with him till his final breath.

So long as the mother faileth to train her children, and start them on a proper way of life, the training which they receive later on will not take its full effect. It is incumbent . . . to provide the mothers with a well-planned program for the education of children, showing how, from infancy, the child must be watched over and taught. These instructions must be given to every mother to serve her as a guide, so that each will train and nurture her children in accordance with the Teachings.

Thus will these young plants in the garden of God's love grow and flourish under the warmth of the Sun of Truth, the gentle spring winds of Heaven, and their mother's guiding hand. Thus, in the Abhá Paradise,* will each become a tree, bearing his clustered fruit, and each one, in this new and wondrous season, out of the bounties of the spring, will become possessed of all beauty and grace.

—'Abdu'l-Bahá

---

* *The Most Glorious Paradise:* the spiritual world beyond this world.

4

O ye loving mothers, know ye that in God's sight, the best of all ways to worship Him is to educate the children and train them in all the perfections of humankind; and no nobler deed than this can be imagined.

—'Abdu'l-Bahá

5

O handmaids of the Lord! . . . Work ye for the guidance of the women in that land, teach the young girls and the children, so that the mothers may educate their little ones from their earliest days, thoroughly train them, rear them to have a goodly character and good morals, guide them to all the virtues of humankind, prevent the development of any behavior that would be worthy of blame, and foster them in the embrace of Bahá'í education.* Thus shall these tender infants be nurtured at the breast of the knowledge of God and His love. Thus shall they grow and flourish, and be taught righteousness and the dignity of humankind, resolution and the will to strive and to endure. Thus shall they learn perseverance in all

---

* Bahá'í education focuses on the spiritual and moral training of children. This is accomplished by educating children on the teachings of the Bahá'í Faith, such as

things, the will to advance, high mindedness and high resolve, chastity and purity of life. Thus shall they be enabled to carry to a successful conclusion whatsoever they undertake.

—*'Abdu'l-Bahá*

6

The great importance attached to the mother's role derives from the fact that she is the *first* educator of the child. Her attitude, her prayers, even what she eats and her physical condition have a great influence on the child when it is still in womb. When the child is born, it is she who has been endowed by God with the milk which is the first food designed for it, and it is intended that, if possible, she should be with the baby to train and nurture it in its earliest days and months. This does not mean that the father does not also love, pray for, and care for his baby, but as he has the primary responsibility of providing for the family, his time to be with his child is usually limited, while the mother is usually closely associated with the baby during this intensely formative time when it is growing and developing faster than it ever will

---

the concept of world citizenship, the elimination of prejudice, the equality of men and women, and the harmony between science and religion.

again during the whole of its life. As the child grows older and more independent, the relative nature of its relationship with its mother and father modifies and the father can play a greater role.

—On behalf of the Universal House of Justice

Expectant Mothers

7

My Lord! My Lord! I praise Thee and I thank Thee for that whereby Thou hast favored Thine humble maidservant, Thy slave beseeching and supplicating Thee, because Thou hast verily guided her unto Thine obvious Kingdom and caused her to hear Thine exalted Call in the contingent world and to behold Thy Signs which prove the appearance of Thy victorious reign over all things.

O my Lord, I dedicate that which is in my womb unto Thee. Then cause it to be a praiseworthy child in Thy Kingdom and a fortunate one by Thy favor and Thy generosity; to develop and to grow up under the charge of Thine education. Verily, Thou art the Gracious! Verily, Thou art the Lord of Great Favor!

—'Abdu'l-Bahá

Nearness to God

1

That the heart is the throne, in which the Revelation of God the All-Merciful is centered, is attested by the holy utterances which We have formerly revealed. Among them is this saying: "Earth and heaven cannot contain Me; what can alone contain Me is the heart of him that believeth in Me, and is faithful to My Cause." How often hath the human heart, which is the recipient of the light of God and the seat of the revelation of the All-Merciful, erred from Him Who is the Source of that light and the Wellspring of that revelation. It is the waywardness of the heart that removeth it far from God, and condemneth it to remoteness from Him. Those hearts, however, that are aware of His Presence, are close to Him, and are to be regarded as having drawn nigh unto His throne.

—Bahá'u'lláh

2

O God! The trials Thou sendest are a salve to the sores of all them who are devoted to Thy will; the remembrance of Thee is a healing medicine to the hearts of such as have drawn nigh unto

Thy court; nearness to Thee is the true life of them who are Thy lovers; Thy presence is the ardent desire of such as yearn to behold Thy face; remoteness from Thee is a torment to those that have acknowledged Thy oneness, and separation from Thee is death unto them that have recognized Thy truth!

I beseech Thee by the sighs which they whose souls pant after Thee have uttered in their remoteness from Thy court, and by the cries of such of Thy lovers as bemoan their separation from Thee, to nourish me with the wine of Thy knowledge and the living waters of Thy love and pleasure. Behold Thy handmaiden, O my Lord, who hath forgotten all else except Thee, and who hath delighted herself with Thy love, and lamented over the things that have befallen Thee at the hands of the wicked doers among Thy creatures. Do Thou ordain for her that which Thou didst ordain for such of Thy handmaidens as circle round the throne of Thy majesty, and gaze, at eventide and at dawn, on Thy beauty.

Thou art, verily, the Lord of the Judgment Day.

—*Bahá'u'lláh*

3

Glory be to Thee, O my God! My face hath been set towards Thy face, and my face is, verily, Thy face, and my call is Thy call, and my

Revelation Thy Revelation, and my self Thy Self, and my Cause Thy Cause, and my behest Thy behest, and my Being Thy Being, and my sovereignty Thy sovereignty, and my glory Thy glory, and my power Thy power.

I implore Thee, O Thou Fashioner of the nations and the King of eternity, to guard Thy handmaidens within the tabernacle of Thy chastity, and to cancel such of their deeds as are unworthy of Thy days. Purge out, then, from them, O my God, all doubts and idle fancies, and sanctify them from whatsoever becometh not their kinship with Thee, O Thou Who art the Lord of names, and the Source of utterance. Thou art He in Whose grasp are the reins of the entire creation.

No God is there but Thee, the Almighty, the Most Exalted, the All-Glorious, the Self-Subsisting.

—Bahá'u'lláh

4

Thine handmaid, O my Lord, hath set her hopes on Thy grace and bounty. Grant that she may obtain that which will draw her nigh unto Thee, and will profit her in every world of Thine. Thou art the Forgiving, the All-Bountiful. There is none other God but Thee, the Ordainer, the Ancient of Days.

Vouchsafe Thy blessings, O Lord, my God, unto them that have quaffed the wine of Thy love be-

fore the face of men, and, in spite of Thine enemies, have acknowledged Thy unity, testified to
Thy oneness, and confessed their belief in that
which hath made the limbs of the oppressors among
Thy creatures to quake, and the flesh of the proud
ones of the earth to tremble. I bear witness that Thy
Sovereignty can never perish, nor Thy Will be al-
tered. Ordain for them that have set their faces towards Thee, and for Thine handmaids that have held
fast by Thy Cord, that which beseemeth the Ocean
of Thy bounty and the Heaven of Thy grace.

—Bahá'u'lláh

5

Lauded be Thy name, O my God and the God
of all things, my Glory and the Glory of all
things, my Desire and the Desire of all things, my
Strength and the Strength of all things, my King
and the King of all things, my Possessor and the
Possessor of all things, my Aim and the Aim of all
things, my Mover and the Mover of all things!
Suffer me not, I implore Thee, to be kept back
from the ocean of Thy tender mercies, nor to be
far removed from the shores of nearness to Thee.

Aught else except Thee, O my Lord, profiteth
me not, and near access to anyone save Thyself
availeth me nothing. I entreat Thee by the plente-
ousness of Thy riches, whereby Thou didst dis-

pense with all else except Thyself, to number me with such as have set their faces towards Thee, and arisen to serve Thee.

Forgive, then, O my Lord, Thy servants and Thy handmaidens. Thou, truly, art the Ever-Forgiving, the Most Compassionate.

—*Bahá'u'lláh*

6

O thou enraptured handmaid of God! Nearness is verily of the soul, not of the body; and the help that is sought, and the help that cometh, is not material but of the spirit; nevertheless it is my hope that thou wilt attain to nearness in every sense. The bounties of God will verily encompass a sanctified soul even as the sun's light doth the moon and stars: be thou assured of this.

—*'Abdu'l-Bahá*

7

O my Lord, my Beloved, my Desire! Befriend me in my loneliness and accompany me in my exile. Remove my sorrow. Cause me to be devoted to Thy beauty. Withdraw me from all else save Thee. Attract me through Thy fragrances of holiness. Cause me to be associated in Thy Kingdom with those who are severed from all else save Thee, who long to serve Thy sacred threshold and who stand to work in Thy

Cause. Enable me to be one of Thy maidservants who have attained to Thy good pleasure. Verily, Thou art the Gracious, the Generous.

—*'Abdu'l-Bahá*

8

O God, my God! These are Thy feeble servants; they are Thy loyal bondsmen and Thy handmaidens, who have bowed themselves down before Thine exalted Utterance and humbled themselves at Thy Threshold of light, and borne witness to Thy oneness through which the Sun hath been made to shine in midday splendor. They have listened to the summons Thou didst raise from out Thy hidden Realm, and with hearts quivering with love and rapture, they have responded to Thy call.

O Lord, shower upon them all the outpourings of Thy mercy, rain down upon them all the waters of Thy grace. Make them to grow as beauteous plants in the garden of heaven, and from the full and brimming clouds of Thy bestowals and out of the deep pools of Thine abounding grace make Thou this garden to flower, and keep it ever green and lustrous, ever fresh and shimmering and fair.

Thou art, verily, the Mighty, the Exalted, the Powerful, He Who alone, in the heavens and on the earth, abideth unchanged. There is none other God save Thee, the Lord of manifest tokens and signs.

—'Abdu'l-Bahá

9

O Lord, my God and my Haven in my distress! My Shield and my Shelter in my woes! My Asylum and Refuge in time of need and in my loneliness my Companion! In my anguish my Solace, and in my solitude a loving Friend! The Remover of the pangs of my sorrows and the Pardoner of my sins!

Wholly unto Thee do I turn, fervently imploring Thee with all my heart, my mind and my tongue, to shield me from all that runs counter to Thy will in this, the cycle of Thy divine unity, and to cleanse me of all defilement that will hinder me from seeking, stainless and unsullied, the shade of the tree of Thy grace.

Have mercy, O Lord, on the feeble, make whole the sick, and quench the burning thirst.

Gladden the bosom wherein the fire of Thy love doth smolder, and set it aglow with the flame of Thy celestial love and spirit.

Robe the tabernacles of divine unity with the vesture of holiness, and set upon my head the crown of Thy favor.

Illumine my face with the radiance of the orb of Thy bounty, and graciously aid me in ministering at Thy holy threshold.

Make my heart overflow with love for Thy creatures and grant that I may become the sign of Thy mercy, the token of Thy grace, the promoter of concord amongst Thy loved ones, devoted unto Thee, uttering Thy commemoration and forgetful of self but ever mindful of what is Thine.

O God, my God! Stay not from me the gentle gales of Thy pardon and grace, and deprive me not of the wellsprings of Thine aid and favor.

'Neath the shade of Thy protecting wings let me nestle, and cast upon me the glance of Thine all-protecting eye.

Loose my tongue to laud Thy name amidst Thy people, that my voice may be raised in great assemblies and from my lips may stream the flood of Thy praise.

Thou art, in all truth, the Gracious, the Glorified, the Mighty, the Omnipotent.

—'Abdu'l-Bahá

Patience

1

And now I implore Thee, by the eternity of Thy Self, to enable me to be patient in these tribulations which have caused the Concourse on high to wail and the denizens of the everlasting Paradise to weep, and through which all faces have been covered with the tawny dust provoked by the anguish that hath seized such of Thy servants as have turned towards Thy Name, the Most Exalted, the Most High. No God is there but Thee, the Almighty, the Inaccessible, the Ever-Forgiving, the Most Compassionate.

—Bahá'u'lláh

2

The virtues and attributes pertaining unto God are all evident and manifest, and have been mentioned and described in all the heavenly Books. Among them are trustworthiness, truthfulness, purity of heart while communing with God, forbearance, resignation to whatever the Almighty hath decreed, contentment with the things His Will hath provided, patience, nay, thankfulness in the midst of tribulation, and complete reliance, in all circumstances, upon Him. These rank, according to the estimate of God, among the highest and most laudable of all acts.

—*Bahá'u'lláh*

3

We render thanks unto God for whatsoever hath befallen Us, and We patiently endure the things He hath ordained in the past or will ordain in the future. In Him have I placed My trust; and into His hands have I committed My Cause. He will, certainly, repay all them that endure with patience and put their confidence in Him. His is the creation and its empire. He exalteth whom He will, and whom He will He doth abase. He shall not be asked of His doings. He, verily, is the All-Glorious, the Almighty.

—*Bahá'u'lláh*

4

For everything there is a sign. The sign of love is fortitude under My decree and patience under My trials.

—*Bahá'u'lláh*

5

O Lord! Verily, we are weak; make us mighty. We are poor; assist us from the treasury of Thy munificence. We are dead; resuscitate us through the breath of the Holy Spirit. We lack patience in tests and in long-suffering; permit us to attain the lights of oneness.

—'Abdu'l-Bahá

6

When faced with the irrevocable decree of the Almighty, the vesture that best befits us in this world is the vesture of patience and submission, and the most meritorious of all deeds is to commit our affairs into His hands and to surrender ourselves to His Will.

—Bahíyyih Khánum

7

O kind Lord! O Comforter of anguished hearts! Send down Thy mercy upon us, and Thy grace, bestow upon us patience, give us the strength to endure. With Thy generous hand, lay Thou a balm upon our sores, grant us a medicine for this never-healing woe. Console Thou Thy loved ones, comfort Thy friends and handmaids, heal Thou our wounded breasts, and with Thy bounty's remedy, restore our festering hearts.

With the gentle breeze of Thy compassion, make fresh and green again these boughs, withered by autumn blasts; restore Thou to flourishing life these flowers, shriveled by the blight of bereavement.

With tidings of the Abhá Paradise,* wed Thou our souls to joy, and rejoice Thou our spirits with heartening voices from the dwellers in the realm of glory.

Thou art the Bounteous, Thou art the Clement; Thou art the Bestower, the Loving.

—*Bahíyyih Khánum*

---

* *The Most Glorious Paradise:* the spiritual world beyond this world.

Peace

1

It is incumbent upon all the peoples of the world to reconcile their differences, and, with perfect unity and peace, abide beneath the shadow of the Tree of His care and loving-kindness.

—Bahá'u'lláh

2

Should the lamp of religion be obscured, chaos and confusion will ensue, and the lights of fairness and justice, of tranquillity and peace cease to shine.

—Bahá'u'lláh

3

With the utmost friendliness and in a spirit of perfect fellowship take ye counsel together, and dedicate the precious days of your lives to the betterment of the world and the promotion of the Cause of Him Who is the Ancient and Sovereign Lord of all.

—Bahá'u'lláh

4

When all mankind shall receive the same opportunity of education and the equality of men and women be realized, the foundations of war will be utterly destroyed. Without equality this will be impossible because all differences and distinction are conducive to discord and strife. Equality between men and women is conducive to the abolition of warfare for the reason that women will never be willing to sanction it. Mothers will not give their sons as sacrifices upon the battlefield after twenty years of anxiety and loving devotion in rearing them from infancy, no matter what cause they are called upon to defend. There is no doubt that when women obtain equality of rights war will entirely cease among mankind.

—'Abdu'l-Bahá

5

The most momentous question of this day is international peace and arbitration, and universal peace is impossible without universal suffrage. Children are educated by the women. The mother bears the troubles and anxieties of rearing the child, undergoes the ordeal of its birth and training. Therefore, it is most difficult for mothers to send to the battlefield those upon whom they have lavished such love and care. Consider a son reared and trained twenty years by a devoted mother. What sleepless nights and restless, anxious days she has spent! Having brought him through dangers and difficulties to the age of maturity, how agonizing then to sacrifice him upon the battlefield! Therefore, the mothers will not sanction war nor be satisfied with it. So it will come to pass that when women participate fully and equally in the affairs of the world, when they enter confidently and capably the great arena of laws and politics, war will cease; for woman will be the obstacle and hindrance to it. This is true and without doubt.

—'Abdu'l-Bahá

6

O handmaid of God, peace must first be established among individuals, until it leadeth in the end to peace among nations. Wherefore . . . strive ye with all your might to create, through the power of the Word of God, genuine love, spiritual communion and durable bonds among individuals. This is your task.

—'Abdu'l-Bahá

7

Woman by nature is opposed to war; she is an advocate of peace. Children are reared and brought up by the mothers who give them the first principles of education and labor assiduously in their behalf. Consider, for instance, a mother who has tenderly reared a son for twenty years to the age of maturity. Surely she will not consent to having that son torn asunder and killed in the field of battle. Therefore, as woman advances toward the degree of man in power and privilege, with the right of vote and control in human government, most assuredly war will cease; for woman is naturally the most devoted and staunch advocate of international peace.

—'Abdu'l-Bahá

8

In past ages humanity has been defective and inefficient because it has been incomplete. War and its ravages have blighted the world; the education of woman will be a mighty step toward its abolition and ending, for she will use her whole influence against war. Woman rears the child and educates the youth to maturity. She will refuse to give her sons for sacrifice upon the field of battle. In truth, she will be the greatest factor in establishing universal peace and international arbitration. Assuredly, woman will abolish warfare among mankind. Inasmuch as human society consists of two parts, the male and female, each the complement of the other, the happiness and stability of humanity cannot be assured unless both are perfected.

—'Abdu'l-Bahá

9

O Thou kind Lord! Thou hast created all humanity from the same stock. Thou hast decreed that all shall belong to the same household. In Thy Holy Presence they are all Thy servants, and all mankind are sheltered beneath Thy Tabernacle; all have gathered together at Thy Table of Bounty; all are illumined through the light of Thy Providence.

O God! Thou art kind to all, Thou hast provided for all, dost shelter all, conferrest life upon all. Thou hast endowed each and all with talents and faculties, and all are submerged in the Ocean of Thy Mercy.

O Thou kind Lord! Unite all. Let the religions agree and make the nations one, so that they may see each other as one family and the whole earth as one home. May they all live together in perfect harmony.

O God! Raise aloft the banner of the oneness of mankind.

O God! Establish the Most Great Peace.

Cement Thou, O God, the hearts together.

O Thou kind Father, God! Gladden our hearts through the fragrance of Thy love. Brighten our eyes through the Light of Thy Guidance. Delight our ears with the melody of Thy Word, and shelter us all in the Stronghold of Thy Providence.

Thou art the Mighty and Powerful, Thou art the Forgiving and Thou art the One Who overlooketh the shortcomings of all mankind.

—'Abdu'l-Bahá

10

The world is in great turmoil, and what is most pathetic is that it has learned to keep away from God, Who alone can save it and alleviate its sufferings. It is our duty, we who have been trusted with the task of applying the divine remedy given by Bahá'u'lláh, to concentrate our attention upon the consummation of this task, and not rest until the peace foretold by the Prophets of God is permanently established.

—On behalf of Shoghi Effendi

11

This [peace] is a matter which vitally affects women, and when they form a conscious and overwhelming mass of public opinion against war there can be no war. . . . They [women] should through teaching and through the active moral support they give to every movement directed towards peace, seek to exert a strong influence on other women's minds in regard to this essential matter.

—*On behalf of Shoghi Effendi*

12

The primary question to be resolved is how the present world, with its entrenched pattern of conflict, can change to a world in which harmony and cooperation will prevail.

World order can be founded only on an unshakable consciousness of the oneness of mankind, a spiritual truth which all the human sciences confirm. Anthropology, physiology, psychology, recognize only one human species, albeit infinitely varied in the secondary aspects of life. Recognition of this truth requires abandonment of prejudice—prejudice of every kind—race, class, color, creed, nation, sex, degree of material civilization, everything which enables people to consider themselves superior to others.

Acceptance of the oneness of mankind is the first fundamental prerequisite for reorganization and administration of the world as one country, the home of humankind. Universal acceptance of this spiritual principle is essential to any successful attempt to establish world peace.

—*Universal House of Justice*

13

The emancipation of women, the achievement of full equality between the sexes, is one of the most important, though less acknowledged prerequisites of peace. The denial of such equality perpetrates an injustice against one half of the world's population and promotes in men harmful attitudes and habits that are carried from the family to the workplace, to political life, and ultimately to international relations. There are no grounds, moral, practical, or biological, upon which such denial can be justified. Only as women are welcomed into full partnership in all fields of human endeavor will the moral and psychological climate be created in which international peace can emerge.

—*Universal House of Justice*

Praise

1

This is the day to make mention of God, to celebrate His praise, and to serve Him; deprive not yourselves thereof. Ye are the letters of the words, and the words of the Book. Ye are the saplings which the hand of Loving-kindness hath planted in the soil of mercy, and which the showers of bounty have made to flourish. He hath protected you from the mighty winds of misbelief, and the tempestuous gales of impiety, and nurtured you with the hands of His loving providence. Now is the time for you to put forth your leaves, and yield your fruit. The fruits of the tree of man have ever been and are goodly deeds and a praiseworthy character.

—Bahá'u'lláh

2

In the Name of God, the Peerless! O handmaid of God! Steadfastness in the Cause is mentioned in the Tablets and set forth by the Pen of the Ancient of Days. Render thanks to the Beloved of the world that thou hast set thy heart on Him and art uttering His praise. Many a man hath in this day been deprived of making mention of the All-Sufficing Lord and of recognizing His truth; and many a woman hath fixed her gaze upon the Horizon of the Most High, and hath adorned herself with the garb of the love of the Desire of the world. This is God's grace which He bestoweth upon whomsoever He pleaseth. By the Daystar of ancient mysteries! The sweet-scented fragrance of every breath breathed in the love of God is wafted in the court of the presence of the Lord of Revelation. The reward of no good deed is or ever will be lost. Blessed art thou, doubly blessed art thou! Thou art reckoned amongst those handmaidens whose love for their kin hath not prevented them from attaining the shores of the Sea of Grace and Mercy. God willing, thou shalt rest eternally neath the shade of the favors of the All-Merciful and shalt be assured of His bounties. Engage in the praise of the True One and rejoice in His loving-kindness.

The world passeth away, and that which is everlasting is the love of God. God willing, thou shalt circumambulate the True One in every world of His worlds and shalt be free from all else save Him.

—*Bahá'u'lláh*

3

In this Day the Blessed Tree of Remembrance speaketh forth in the Kingdom of Utterance saying: Well is it with the servant who hath turned his face towards Him, and embraced His truth, and with the handmaiden who hath hearkened to His Voice and become of the blissful. Verily, she is a champion of the field of true understanding. To this the Tongue of Truth beareth witness from His exalted Station.

O My leaf, blessed art thou for having responded to My call when it was raised in the name of the True One. Thou didst recognize My Revelation when men of renown were immersed in manifest idle fancies. Thou hast verily attained the mercy of thy Lord time and again. Render thanks unto Him and glorify Him with thy Praise. He is, in truth, with His handmaidens and servants who have turned towards Him. The shining glory from the Horizon of My Kingdom be upon thee and upon the one who hath guided thee to My straight path.

—*Bahá'u'lláh*

4

Praise, immeasurable praise be to Thee! I swear by Thy glory! My inner and outer tongue, openly and secretly, testify that Thou hast been exalted above the reach and ken of Thy creatures, above the utterance of Thy servants, above the testimonies of Thy dear ones and Thy chosen ones, and the apprehension of Thy Prophets and of Thy Messengers.

I beseech Thee, O my Lord, by Thy Name which Thou hast made to be the Day-Spring of Thy Revelation and the Dawning-Place of Thine inspiration, to ordain for this wronged One and for them that are dear to Thee what becometh Thy loftiness. Thou, in very truth, art the All-Bountiful, the All-Powerful, the All-Knowing, the All-Wise.

—*Bahá'u'lláh*

5

Every existence, whether seen or unseen, O my Lord, testifieth that Thy mercy hath surpassed all created things, and Thy loving-kindness embraced the entire creation. Look upon them, I entreat Thee, with the eyes of Thy mercy. Thou art the Ever-Forgiving, the Most Compassionate. Do with them as beseemeth Thy glory, and Thy majesty, and Thy greatness, and Thy bounteousness and Thy grace. Deal not with them according to the limitations imposed upon them, or the manifold vicissitudes of their earthly life.

Thou knowest, O my Lord, that I am but one of Thy servants. I have tasted of the sweetness of Thy speech, and acknowledged Thy unity and Thy singleness, and set my face towards the Source of Thy most excellent names and the Day-Spring of Thy transcendent attributes, and wished to be enabled by Thee to immerse myself beneath the ocean of Thy oneness and to be submerged by the mighty waters of Thy unity.

Assist me, by Thy strengthening grace, O my Lord, to do what Thou didst will, and withhold not from me the things Thou dost possess. So enravish me with the wonders of Thine utterances that the noise and distraction of this world may be powerless to deter me from turning unto Thee, and may fail to shake my constancy in Thy Cause, or to distract my gaze from the horizon of Thy grace. Aid me, then, O my God, to do what pleaseth Thee, and to carry out Thy will. Write down for me, moreover, the good of this world and of the world which is to come, and ordain for me a seat of truth in Thy presence. Potent art Thou to do what Thou willest, and to rule as Thou pleasest. No God is there but Thee, the Inaccessible, the All-Glorious, the Most Great.

All praise to Thee, O Lord of the worlds and the Object of the adoration of the entire creation!

—*Bahá'u'lláh*

6

O thou handmaid of God! In this day, to thank God for His bounties consisteth in possessing a radiant heart, and a soul open to the promptings of the spirit. This is the essence of thanksgiving.

—*'Abdu'l-Bahá*

7

O Thou Kind Bestower, O Nourisher of our souls and hearts!

We have no aim, except to walk Thy path; we have no wish, except to bring Thee joy. Our souls are united, and our hearts are welded, each to each. In offering Thee our thanks and praise, in following Thy ways and soaring in Thy skies, we are all one.

We are helpless, stand Thou by us, and give us strength.

Thou art the Protector, the Provider, the Kind.

—*Bahíyyih Khánum*

Protection

1

L auded be Thy name, O Lord my God! I entreat Thee by Thy Name through which the Hour hath struck, and the Resurrection came to pass, and fear and trembling seized all that are in heaven and all that are on earth, to rain down, out of the heaven of Thy mercy and the clouds of Thy tender compassion, what will gladden the hearts of Thy servants, who have turned towards Thee and helped Thy Cause.

Keep safe Thy servants and Thy handmaidens, O my Lord, from the darts of idle fancy and vain imaginings, and give them from the hands of thy grace a draught of the soft-flowing waters of Thy knowledge.

Thou, truly, art the Almighty, the Most Exalted, the Ever-Forgiving, the Most Generous.

—Bahá'u'lláh

2

O Thou, at Whose dreadful majesty all things have trembled, in Whose grasp are the affairs of all men, towards Whose grace and mercy are set the faces of all Thy creatures! I entreat Thee, by

Thy Name which Thou hast ordained to be the spirit of all names that are in the kingdom of names, to shield us from the whisperings of those who have turned away from Thee, and have repudiated the truth of Thy most august and most exalted Self, in this Revelation that hath caused the kingdom of Thy names to tremble.

I am one of Thy handmaidens, O my Lord! I have turned my face towards the sanctuary of Thy gracious favors and the adored tabernacle of Thy glory. Purify me of all that is not of Thee, and strengthen me to love Thee and to fulfill Thy pleasure, that I may delight myself in the contemplation of Thy beauty, and be rid of all attachment to any of Thy creatures, and may, at every moment, proclaim: "Magnified be God, the Lord of the worlds!"

Let my food, O my Lord, be Thy beauty, and my drink the light of Thy presence, and my hope Thy pleasure, and my work Thy praise, and my companion Thy remembrance, and my aid Thy sovereignty, and my dwelling-place Thy habitation, and my home the seat which Thou hast exalted above the limitations of them that are shut out as by a veil from Thee.

Thou art, in truth, the God of power, of strength and glory.

—*Bahá'u'lláh*

3

Thou seest, O my God, how the wrongs committed by such of Thy creatures as have turned their backs to Thee have come in between Him in Whom Thy Godhead is manifest and Thy servants. Send down upon them, O my Lord, what will cause them to be busied with each others' concerns. Let, then, their violence be confined to their own selves, that the land and they that dwell therein may find peace.

One of Thy handmaidens, O my Lord, hath sought Thy face, and soared in the atmosphere of Thy pleasure. Withhold not from her, O my Lord, the things Thou didst ordain for the chosen ones among Thy handmaidens. Enable her, then, to be so attracted by Thine utterances that she will celebrate Thy praise amongst them.

Potent art Thou to do what pleaseth Thee. No God is there but Thee, the Almighty, Whose help is implored by all men.

—*Bahá'u'lláh*

4

Magnified art Thou, O Lord my God! I ask Thee by Thy Name which Thou hast set up above all other names, through which the veil of heaven hath been split asunder and the Daystar of

Thy beauty hath risen above the horizon, shining with the brightness of Thy Name, the Exalted, the Most High, to succor me with Thy wondrous help and to preserve me in the shelter of Thy care and protection.

I am one of Thy handmaidens, O my Lord! Unto Thee have I turned, and in Thee have I placed my trust. Grant that I may be so confirmed in my love for Thee, and in fulfilling that which is well-pleasing unto Thee, that neither the defection of the infidels among Thy people, nor the clamor of the hypocrites among Thy creatures, may avail to keep me back from Thee.

Purge Thou mine ear, O my Lord, that I may hearken unto the verses sent down unto Thee, and illuminate my heart with the light of Thy knowledge, and loose my tongue that it may make mention of Thee and sing Thy praise. By Thy might, O my God! My soul is wedded to none beside Thee, and my heart seeketh none except Thine own Self.

No God is there beside Thee, the All-Glorious, the Great Giver, the Forgiving, the Compassionate.

—*Bahá'u'lláh*

5

Glorified art Thou, O Lord my God! Thou art He the fire of Whose love hath set ablaze the hearts of them who have recognized Thy unity, and the splendors of Whose countenance have illuminated the faces of such as have drawn nigh unto Thy court. How plenteous, O my God, is the stream of Thy knowledge! . . .

I beseech Thee, by Thy name through which Thou turnest restlessness into tranquillity, fear into confidence, weakness into strength, and abasement into glory, that Thou of Thy grace wilt aid me and Thy servants to exalt Thy name, to deliver Thy Message, and to proclaim Thy Cause. . .

I am, O my Lord, Thy handmaiden, who hath hearkened to Thy call, and hastened unto Thee, fleeing from herself and resting her heart upon Thee. I implore Thee, O my Lord, by Thy name out of which all the treasures of the earth were brought forth, to shield me from the hints of such as have disbelieved in Thee and repudiated Thy truth.

Powerful art Thou to do what Thou pleasest. Thou art, verily, the All-Knowing, the All-Wise.

—*Bahá'u'lláh*

Qualities of Women

1

He is effulgent from the all-highest Horizon.
O My handmaid! Throughout the centuries
and ages many a man hath waited expectant for
God's Revelation, and yet when the Light shone
forth from the horizon of the world, all but a few
turned their faces away from it. Whosoever from
amongst the handmaidens hath recognized the
Lord of all Names is recorded in the Book as one
of those men by the Pen of the Most High. Offer
thou praise to the Beloved of the world for having
aided thee to recognize the Dayspring of His Signs
and the Revealer of the evidences of His Glory.
This is a great bounty, a bounteous favor. Preserve
it in the name of the True One.

—Bahá'u'lláh

2

By My Life! The names of handmaidens who
are devoted to God are written and set down
by the Pen of the Most High in the Crimson Book.
They excel over men in the sight of God.

—Bahá'u'lláh

3

We beseech the True One to adorn His handmaidens with the ornament of chastity, of trustworthiness, of righteousness and of purity. Verily, He is the All-Bestowing, the All-Generous. We make mention of the handmaidens of God at this time and announce unto them the glad-tidings of the tokens of the mercy and compassion of God and His consideration for them, glorified be He, and We supplicate Him for all His assistance to perform such deeds as are the cause of the exaltation of His Word. He verily speaketh the truth and enjoineth upon His servants and His handmaidens that which will profit them in every world of His worlds. He, verily, is the All-Forgiving, the All-Merciful.

—*Bahá'u'lláh*

4

O Handmaids of the Self-Sustaining Lord! Exert your efforts so that you may attain the honor and privilege ordained for women. Undoubtedly the greatest glory of women is servitude at His Threshold and submissiveness at His door; it is the possession of a vigilant heart, and praise of the incomparable God; it is heartfelt love towards other handmaids and spotless chastity; it is obedience to and consideration for their husbands and the education and care of their children; and it is tranquillity, and dignity, perseverance in the remembrance of the Lord, and the utmost enkindlement and attraction.

—*On behalf of the Universal House of Justice*

5

From the beginning of existence until the Promised Day men retained superiority over women in every respect. It is revealed in the Qur'án: "Men have superiority over women." But in this wondrous Dispensation,* the supreme outpouring of the Glorious Lord became the cause of manifest achievements by women. Some handmaidens arose who excelled men in the arena of knowledge. They arose with such love and spirituality that they became the cause of the outpouring of the bounty of the Sovereign Lord upon mankind, and with their sanctity, purity and attributes of the spirit led a great many to the shore of unity. They became a guiding torch to the wanderers in the wastes

---

* A dispensation is the period of time during which the laws and teachings of a Prophet of God have spiritual authority. The dispensation of Bahá'u'lláh began in 1852, when He experienced the first intimation of His mission, and will last until the advent of the next Manifestation of God, which Bahá'u'lláh asserts will occur in no less than one thousand years.

of bewilderment, and enkindled the despondent in the nether world with the flame of the love of the Lord. This is a bounteous characteristic of this wondrous Age which hath granted strength to the weaker sex and hath bestowed masculine might upon womanhood.

—'Abdu'l-Bahá

6

The handmaidens of God and the bondsmaids in His divine Court should reveal such attributes and attitudes amongst the women of the world as would cause them to stand out and achieve renown in the circles of women. That is, they should associate with them with supreme chastity and steadfast decency, with unshakable faith, articulate speech, an eloquent tongue, irrefutable testimony and high resolve. Beseech God that thou mayest attain unto all these bounties.

—'Abdu'l-Bahá

7

Therefore, strive to show in the human world that women are most capable and efficient, that their hearts are more tender and susceptible than the hearts of men, that they are more philanthropic and responsive toward the needy and suffering, that they are inflexibly opposed to war and are lovers of peace. Strive that the ideal of international peace may become realized through the efforts of womankind, for man is more inclined to war than woman, and a real evidence of woman's superiority will be her service and efficiency in the establishment of universal peace.

—'Abdu'l-Bahá

8

The woman is indeed of the greater importance to the race. She has the greater burden and the greater work. Look at the vegetable and the animal worlds. The palm which carries the fruit is the tree most prized by the date grower. The Arab knows that for a long journey the mare has the longest wind. For her greater strength and fierceness, the lioness is more feared by the hunter than the lion. . . .

The woman has greater moral courage than the man; she has also special gifts which enable her to govern in moments of danger and crisis. If necessary she can become a warrior.

—'Abdu'l-Bahá

9

In some respects woman is superior to man. She is more tender-hearted, more receptive, her intuition is more intense.

—'Abdu'l-Bahá

165

10

The world in the past has been ruled by force, and man has dominated over women by reason of his more forceful and aggressive qualities both of body and mind. But the balance is already shifting—force is losing its weight and mental alertness, intuition, and the spiritual qualities of love and service, in which woman is strong, are gaining ascendancy. Hence the new age will be an age, less masculine, and more permeated with the feminine ideals—or, to speak more exactly, will be an age in which the masculine and feminine elements of civilization will be more evenly balanced.

—'Abdu'l-Bahá

11

Exert yourselves, that haply ye may be enabled to acquire such virtues as shall honor and distinguish you amongst all women. Of a surety, there is no greater pride and glory for a woman than to be a handmaid in God's Court of Grandeur; and the qualities that shall merit her this station are an alert and wakeful heart; a firm conviction of the unity of God, the Peerless; a heartfelt love for all His maidservants; spotless purity and chastity; obedience to and consideration for her husband; attention to the education and nurturing of her children; composure, calmness, dignity and self-possession;

diligence in praising God, and worshipping Him both night and day; constancy and firmness in His holy Covenant;* and the utmost ardor, enthusiasm, and attachment to His Cause.

—'Abdu'l-Bahá

12

O thou maidservant of God! Every woman who becometh the maidservant of God outshineth in glory the empresses of the world, for she is related to God, and her sovereignty is everlasting, whereas a handful of dust will obliterate the name and fame of those empresses. In other words, as soon as they go down to the grave they are reduced to naught. The maidservants of God's Kingdom, on the other hand, enjoy eternal sovereignty unaffected by the passing of ages and generations.

Consider how many empresses have come and gone since the time of Christ. Each was the ruler of a country but now all trace and name of them is lost, while Mary Magdalene, who was only a peasant and a maidservant of God, still shineth from the horizon of everlasting glory. Strive thou, therefore, to remain the maidservant of God.

—'Abdu'l-Bahá

---

* The binding agreement between God and humanity that God will provide guidance to humankind and that humankind will accept it.

Service

1

Wert thou to consider this world, and realize how fleeting are the things that pertain unto it, thou wouldst choose to tread no path except the path of service to the Cause of thy Lord. None would have the power to deter thee from celebrating His praise . . .

Go thou straight on and persevere in His service. Say: O people! The Day, promised unto you in all the Scriptures, is now come. Fear ye God, and withhold not yourselves from recognizing the One Who is the Object of your creation. Hasten ye unto Him. Better is this for you than the world and all that is therein. Would that ye could perceive it!

—*Bahá'u'lláh*

2

I magnify Thy Name, O my God, and offer thanksgiving unto Thee, O my Desire, inasmuch as Thou hast enabled me to clearly perceive Thy straight Path, hast unveiled Thy Great Announcement before mine eyes and hast aided me to set my face towards the Dayspring of Thy Revelation and the Fountainhead of Thy Cause, whilst Thy servants and Thy people turned away from Thee. I entreat Thee, O Lord of the Kingdom of eternity, by the shrill voice of the Pen of Glory, and by the Burning Fire which calleth aloud from the verdant Tree, and by the Ark which Thou hast specially chosen for the people of Bahá,* to grant that I may remain steadfast in my love for Thee, be well pleased with whatsoever Thou hast prescribed for me in Thy Book and may stand firm in Thy service and in the service of Thy loved ones. Graciously assist then Thy servants, O my God, to do that which will serve to exalt Thy Cause and will enable them to observe whatsoever Thou hast revealed in Thy Book.

Verily Thou art the Lord of Strength, Thou art potent to ordain whatsoever Thou willest and within Thy grasp Thou holdest the reins of all created things. No God is there but Thee, the All-Powerful, the All-Knowing, the All-Wise.

—Bahá'u'lláh

3

Be generous in prosperity, and thankful in adversity. Be worthy of the trust of thy neighbor, and look upon him with a bright and friendly face.

---

* Bahá'ís.

Be a treasure to the poor, an admonisher to the rich, an answerer of the cry of the needy, a preserver of the sanctity of thy pledge. Be fair in thy judgment, and guarded in thy speech. Be unjust to no man, and show all meekness to all men. Be as a lamp unto them that walk in darkness, a joy to the sorrowful, a sea for the thirsty, a haven for the distressed, an upholder and defender of the victim of oppression. Let integrity and uprightness distinguish all thine acts. Be a home for the stranger, a balm to the suffering, a tower of strength for the fugitive. Be eyes to the blind, and a guiding light unto the feet of the erring. Be an ornament to the countenance of truth, a crown to the brow of fidelity, a pillar of the temple of righteousness, a breath of life to the body of mankind, an ensign of the hosts of justice, a luminary above the horizon of virtue, a dew to the soil of the human heart, an ark on the ocean of knowledge, a sun in the heaven of bounty, a gem on the diadem of wisdom, a shining light in the firmament of thy generation, a fruit upon the tree of humility.

—*Bahá'u'lláh*

4

Think ye at all times of rendering some service to every member of the human race.

—*'Abdu'l-Bahá*

5

Those souls who are of the Kingdom eagerly wish to be of service to the poor, to sympathize with them, to show kindness to the miserable and to make their lives fruitful.

—'Abdu'l-Bahá

6

Wherefore, rest ye neither day nor night and seek no ease. Tell ye the secrets of servitude, follow the pathway of service, till ye attain the promised succor that cometh from the realms of God.

—'Abdu'l-Bahá

7

O my spiritual loved ones! Praise be to God, ye have thrust the veils aside and recognized the compassionate Beloved, and have hastened away from this abode to the placeless realm. Ye have pitched your tents in the world of God, and to glorify Him, the Self-Subsistent, ye have raised sweet voices and sung songs that pierced the heart. Well done! A thousand times well done! For ye have beheld the Light made manifest, and in your reborn beings ye have raised the cry, "Blessed be the Lord, the best of all creators!" Ye were but babes in the womb, then were ye sucklings, and from a precious breast ye drew the milk of knowledge, then came ye to your full growth, and won salvation. Now is the time for service, and for servitude unto the Lord. Release yourselves from all distracting thoughts, deliver the Message with an eloquent tongue, adorn your assemblages with praise of the Beloved, till bounty shall descend in overwhelming floods and dress the world in fresh greenery and blossoms. This streaming bounty is even the counsels, admonitions, instructions, and injunctions of Almighty God.

—'Abdu'l-Bahá

Steadfastness

1

L auded be Thy name, O my God! Aid Thou by
Thy strengthening grace Thy servants and Thy
handmaidens to recount Thy virtues and to be steadfast in their love towards Thee. How many the leaves
which the tempests of trials have caused to fall, and
how many, too, are those which, clinging tenaciously
to the tree of Thy Cause, have remained unshaken
by the tests that have assailed them, O Thou Who
art our Lord, the Most Merciful!

I render Thee thanks that Thou hast made known
unto me such servants as have utterly abolished, by
the power of Thy might and of Thy sovereignty,
the idols of their corrupt desires, and were not kept
back by the things which are possessed by Thy creatures from turning in the direction of Thy grace.
These have so vehemently rent the veils asunder that
the dwellers of the cities of self have wept, and fear
and trembling seized the people of envy and wick-
edness who, adorning their heads and their bodies
with the emblems of knowledge, have proudly re-
jected Thee and turned away from Thy beauty.

I implore Thee, O my Lord, by Thy surpassing
majesty and Thine Ancient Name, to enable Thy

loved ones to assist Thee. Direct, then, continually their faces towards Thy face, and write down for them what will cause all hearts to exult and all eyes to be gladdened.

Thou, truly, art the Help in peril, the Self-Subsisting.

—*Bahá'u'lláh*

2

The spirit that animateth the human heart is the knowledge of God, and its truest adorning is the recognition of the truth that "He doeth whatsoever He willeth, and ordaineth that which He pleaseth." Its raiment is the fear of God, and its perfection steadfastness in His Faith. Thus God instructeth whosoever seeketh Him. He, verily, loveth the one that turneth towards Him. There is none other God but Him, the Forgiving, the Most Bountiful. All praise be to God, the Lord of all worlds.

—*Bahá'u'lláh*

3

O Thou Whose nearness is my wish, Whose presence is my hope, Whose remembrance is my desire, Whose court of glory is my goal, Whose abode is my aim, Whose name is my healing, Whose love is the radiance of my heart, Whose service is my highest aspiration! I beseech Thee by Thy Name, through which Thou hast enabled them that have recognized Thee to soar to the sublimest heights of the knowledge of Thee and empowered such as devoutly worship Thee to ascend into the precincts of the court of Thy holy favors, to aid me to turn my face towards Thy face, to fix mine eyes upon Thee, and to speak of Thy glory.

I am the one, O my Lord, who hath forgotten all else but Thee, and turned towards the Dayspring of Thy grace, who hath forsaken all save Thyself in the hope of drawing nigh unto Thy court. Behold me, then, with mine eyes lifted up towards the Seat that shineth with the splendors of the light of Thy Face. Send down, then, upon me, O my Beloved, that which will enable me to be steadfast in Thy Cause, so that the doubts of the infidels may not hinder me from turning towards Thee.

Thou art, verily, the God of Power, the Help in Peril, the All-Glorious, the Almighty.

—*Bahá'u'lláh*

4

I implore Thee, O my God and my Master, by Thy word through which they who have believed in Thy unity have soared up into the atmosphere of Thy knowledge, and they who are devoted to Thee have ascended into the heaven of Thy oneness, to inspire Thy loved ones with that which will assure their hearts in Thy Cause. Endue them with such steadfastness that nothing whatsoever will hinder them from turning towards Thee.

Thou art, verily, the Bountiful, the Munificent, the Forgiving, the Compassionate.

—*Bahá'u'lláh*

5

O compassionate God! Thanks be to Thee for Thou hast awakened and made me conscious. Thou hast given me a seeing eye and favored me with a hearing ear, hast led me to Thy kingdom and guided me to Thy path. Thou hast shown me the right way and caused me to enter the ark of deliverance. O God! Keep me steadfast and make me firm and staunch. Protect me from violent tests and preserve and shelter me in the strongly fortified fortress of Thy Covenant and Testament. Thou art the Powerful. Thou art the Seeing. Thou art the Hearing.

O Thou the Compassionate God. Bestow upon me a heart which, like unto a glass, may be illumined with the light of Thy love, and confer upon me thoughts which may change this world into a rose garden through the outpourings of heavenly grace.

Thou art the Compassionate, the Merciful. Thou art the Great Beneficent God.

—*'Abdu'l-Bahá*

6

O Lord my God! Assist Thy loved ones to be firm in Thy Faith, to walk in Thy ways, to be steadfast in Thy Cause. Give them Thy grace to withstand the onslaught of self and passion, to follow the light of divine guidance. Thou art the Powerful, the Gracious, the Self-Subsisting, the Bestower, the Compassionate, the Almighty, the All-Bountiful.

—*'Abdu'l-Bahá*

7

All the virtues of humankind are summed up in the one word "steadfastness," if we but act according to its laws. It draws to us as by a magnet the blessings and bestowals of Heaven, if we but rise up according to the obligations it implies.

God be praised, the house of the heart is lit by the light of unswerving constancy, and the soul's lodging is bedecked with the ornament of faithfulness.

Steadfastness is a treasure that makes a man so rich as to have no need of the world or any person or any thing that is therein. Constancy is a special joy, that leads us mortals on to lofty heights, great progress, and the winning of the perfections of Heaven. All praise be to the Beloved's holy court, for granting this most wondrous grace to His faithful people, and to His favored ones, this best of gifts.

—*Bahíyyih Khánum*

Suffering and Difficulties

1

Glory be to Thee, O my God! I beg of Thee by Thy name, the Most Merciful, to protect Thy servants and Thy handmaidens when the tempests of trials pass over them, and Thy manifold tests assail them. Enable them, then, O my God, so to seek refuge within the stronghold of Thy love and of Thy Revelation, that neither Thine adversaries nor the wicked doers among Thy servants, who have broken Thy Covenant and Thy Testament, and turned away most disdainfully from the Dayspring of Thine Essence and the Revealer of Thy glory, may prevail against them.

They themselves, O my Lord, have waited at the door of Thy grace. Do Thou open it to their faces with the keys of Thy bountiful favors. Potent art Thou to do what Thou willest, and to ordain what Thou pleasest. These are the ones, O my Lord, who have set their faces towards Thee, and turned unto Thy habitation. Do with them, therefore, as becometh Thy mercy, which hath surpassed the worlds.

—Bahá'u'lláh

2

O Thou Whose tests are a healing medicine to such as are nigh unto Thee, Whose sword is the ardent desire of all them that love Thee, Whose dart is the dearest wish of those hearts that yearn after Thee, Whose decree is the sole hope of them that have recognized Thy truth! I implore Thee, by Thy divine sweetness and by the splendors of the glory of Thy face, to send down upon us from Thy retreats on high that which will enable us to draw nigh unto Thee. Set, then, our feet firm, O my God, in Thy Cause, and enlighten our hearts with the effulgence of Thy knowledge, and illumine our breasts with the brightness of Thy names.

—*Bahá'u'lláh*

3

Dispel my grief by Thy bounty and Thy generosity, O God, my God, and banish mine anguish through Thy sovereignty and Thy might. Thou seest me, O my God, with my face set towards Thee at a time when sorrows have compassed me on every side. I implore Thee, O Thou Who art the Lord of all being, and overshadowest all things visible and invisible, by Thy Name whereby Thou hast subdued the hearts and the souls of men, and by the billows of the Ocean of Thy mercy and the splendors of the Daystar of Thy bounty, to number me with them whom nothing whatsoever hath deterred from setting their faces toward Thee, O Thou Lord of all names and Maker of the heavens!

Thou beholdest, O my Lord, the things which have befallen me in Thy days. I entreat Thee, by Him Who is the Dayspring of Thy names and the Dawning-Place of Thine attributes, to ordain for me what will enable me to arise to serve Thee and to extol Thy virtues. Thou art, verily, the Almighty, the Most Powerful, Who art wont to answer the prayers of all men!

And, finally, I beg of Thee by the light of Thy countenance to bless my affairs, and redeem my debts, and satisfy my needs. Thou art He to Whose power and to Whose dominion every tongue hath testified, and Whose majesty and Whose sovereignty every understanding heart hath acknowledged. No God is there but Thee, Who hearest and art ready to answer.

—*Bahá'u'lláh*

4

Lauded be Thy name, O my God! Thou beholdest how the tempestuous winds of tests have caused the steadfast in faith to tremble, and how the breath of trials hath stirred up those whose hearts had been firmly established, except such as have partaken of the Wine that is life indeed from the hands of the Manifestation of Thy name, the Most Merciful. These are the ones whom no word except Thy most exalted word can move, whom nothing whatever save the sweet smelling fragrance of the robe of Thy remembrance can enrapture, O Thou Who art the Possessor of all names and the Maker of earth and heaven!

I implore Thee, O Thou Who art the beloved Companion of Bahá, by Thy name, the All-Glorious, to keep safe these Thy servants under the shadow of the wings of Thine all-encompassing mercy, that the darts of the evil suggestions of the wicked doers among Thy creatures, who have disbelieved in Thy signs, may be kept back from them. No one on earth, O my Lord, can withstand Thy power, and none in all the kingdom of Thy names is able to frustrate Thy purpose. Show forth, then, the power of Thy sovereignty and of Thy dominion, and teach Thy loved ones what beseemeth them in Thy days.

Thou art, verily, the Almighty, the Most Exalted, the All-Glorious, the Most Great.

—*Bahá'u'lláh*

5

Is there any Remover of difficulties save God? Say: Praised be God! He is God! All are His servants, and all abide by His bidding!

—*The Báb*

6

O thou who hast bowed thyself down in prayer before the Kingdom of God! Blessed art thou, for the beauty of the divine Countenance hath enraptured thy heart, and the light of inner wisdom hath filled it full, and within it shineth the brightness of the Kingdom. Know thou that God is with thee under all conditions, and that He guardeth thee from the changes and chances of this world and hath made thee a handmaid in His mighty vineyard.

—'Abdu'l-Bahá

7

Convey thou unto the handmaids of the Merciful the message that when a test turneth violent they must stand unmoved, and faithful to their love for Bahá.* In winter come the storms, and the great winds blow, but then will follow spring in all its beauty, adorning hill and plain with perfumed plants and red anemones, fair to see. Then will the birds trill out upon the branches their songs of joy, and sermonize in lilting tones from the pulpits of the trees. Erelong shall ye bear witness that the lights are streaming forth, the banners of the realm above are waving, the sweet scents of the All-Merciful are wafted abroad, the hosts of the Kingdom are

---

* Bahá'u'lláh.

marching down, the angels of heaven are rushing forward, and the Holy Spirit is breathing upon all those regions. On that day thou shalt behold the waverers, men and women alike, frustrated of their hopes and in manifest loss. This is decreed by the Lord, the Revealer of Verses.

As to thee, blessed art thou, for thou art steadfast in the Cause of God, firm in His Covenant.* I beg of Him to bestow upon thee a spiritual soul, and the life of the Kingdom, and to make thee a leaf verdant and flourishing on the Tree of Life, that thou mayest serve the handmaids of the Merciful with spirituality and good cheer.

Thy generous Lord will assist thee to labor in His vineyard and will cause thee to be the means of spreading the spirit of unity among His handmaids. He will make thine inner eye to see with the light of knowledge, He will forgive thy sins and transform them into goodly deeds. Verily He is the Forgiving, the Compassionate, the Lord of immeasurable grace.

—'Abdu'l-Bahá

---

* The binding agreement between God and humanity that God will provide guidance to humankind and that humankind will accept it.

8

O thou handmaid aflame with the fire of God's love! Grieve thou not over the troubles and hardships of this nether world, nor be thou glad in times of ease and comfort, for both shall pass away. This present life is even as a swelling wave, or a mirage, or drifting shadows. Could ever a distorted image on the desert serve as refreshing waters? No, by the Lord of Lords! Never can reality and the mere semblance of reality be one, and wide is the difference between fancy and fact, between truth and the phantom thereof.

Know thou that the Kingdom is the real world, and this nether place is only its shadow stretching out. A shadow hath no life of its own; its existence is only a fantasy, and nothing more; it is but images reflected in water, and seeming as pictures to the eye.

Rely upon God. Trust in Him. Praise Him, and call Him continually to mind. He verily turneth trouble into ease, and sorrow into solace, and toil into utter peace. He verily hath dominion over all things.

If thou wouldst hearken to my words, release thyself from the fetters of whatsoever cometh to pass. Nay rather, under all conditions thank thou thy loving Lord, and yield up thine affairs unto His Will that worketh as He pleaseth. This verily is better for thee than all else, in either world.

—'Abdu'l-Bahá

9

To the loyal soul, a test is but God's grace and favor; for the valiant doth joyously press forward to furious battle on the field of anguish, when the coward, whimpering with fright, will tremble and shake. So too, the proficient student, who hath with great competence mastered his subjects and committed them to memory, will happily exhibit his skills before his examiners on the day of his tests. So too will solid gold wondrously gleam and shine out in the assayer's fire.

It is clear, then, that tests and trials are, for sanctified souls, but God's bounty and grace, while to the weak, they are a calamity, unexpected and sudden.

These tests . . . do but cleanse the spotting of self from off the mirror of the heart, till the Sun of Truth can cast its rays thereon . . .

—'Abdu'l-Bahá

10

From time immemorial even to this day the chosen ones of God have always been exposed to the woes and sufferings that the disdainful have inflicted upon them. They have been made the targets of the darts and spears of hatred and enmity that the heedless have unloosed upon them. Yet it is clear and evident that the loved ones of God will always, with the whole affection of their hearts and souls, welcome every tribulation in the path of the peerless Beloved and will, with utmost joy and love, accept the pain of every grievous wound for the sake of the incomparable One. Far from grieving or complaining, they offer praise and thanksgiving to Him Who is the Sovereign Lord of all. They commit their affairs to the care of the Lord of all mankind and surrender everything to Him Whose power is irresistible. He is the Potent, the Powerful, the Avenger, the All-Compelling.

—*Baháyyih Khánum*

Trust in God

1

Lauded and glorified art thou, O my God! I entreat Thee by the sighing of Thy lovers and by the tears shed by them that long to behold Thee, not to withhold from me Thy tender mercies in Thy Day, nor to deprive me of the melodies of the Dove that extolleth Thy oneness before the light that shineth from thy face. I am the one who is in misery, O God! Behold me cleaving fast to Thy Name, the All-Possessing. I am the one who is sure to perish; behold me clinging to Thy Name, the Imperishable. I implore Thee, therefore, by Thy Self, the Exalted, the Most High, not to abandon me unto mine own self and unto the desires of a corrupt inclination. Hold Thou my hand with the hand of Thy power, and deliver me from the depths of my fancies and idle imaginings, and cleanse me of all that is abhorrent unto Thee.

Cause me, then, to turn wholly unto Thee, to put my whole trust in Thee, to seek Thee as my Refuge, and to flee unto Thy face. Thou art, verily, He Who, through the power of His might, doeth whatsoever He desireth, and commandeth, through the potency of His will, whatsoever He chooseth. None can withstand the operation of Thy decree; none can divert the course of Thine appointment. Thou art, in truth, the Almighty, the All-Glorious, the Most Bountiful.

—Bahá'u'lláh

2

Be fair to yourselves and to others, that the evidences of justice may be revealed, through your deeds, among Our faithful servants. Beware lest ye encroach upon the substance of your neighbor. Prove yourselves worthy of his trust and confidence in you, and withhold not from the poor the gifts which the grace of God hath bestowed upon you. He, verily, shall recompense the charitable, and doubly repay them for what they have bestowed. No God is there but Him. All creation and its empire are His. He bestoweth His gifts on whom He will, and from whom He will He withholdeth them. He is the Great Giver, the Most Generous, the Benevolent.

—Bahá'u'lláh

3

Arise to aid thy Lord at all times and in all circumstances, and be thou one of His helpers. Admonish, then, the people to lend a hearing ear to the words which the Spirit of God hath uttered in this irradiant and resplendent Tablet. Say: Sow not, O people, the seeds of dissension amongst men, and contend not with your neighbor. Be patient under all conditions, and place your whole trust and confidence in God. Aid ye your Lord with the sword of wisdom and of utterance.

—Bahá'u'lláh

4

Let the fear of no one dismay thee. Trust in the Lord, thy God, for He is sufficient unto whosoever trusteth in Him. He, verily, shall protect thee, and in Him shalt thou abide in safety.

—Bahá'u'lláh

5

The source of all good is trust in God, submission unto His command, and contentment with His holy will and pleasure.

—Bahá'u'lláh

6

Purge thou thy heart that We may cause fountains of wisdom and utterance to gush out therefrom, thus enabling thee to raise thy voice among all mankind. Unloose thy tongue and proclaim the truth for the sake of the remembrance of thy merciful Lord. Be not afraid of anyone, place thy whole trust in God, the Almighty, the All-Knowing.

—*Bahá'u'lláh*

7

Whatever hath befallen you, hath been for the sake of God. This is the truth, and in this there is no doubt. You should, therefore, leave all your affairs in His Hands, place your trust in Him, and rely upon Him. He will assuredly not forsake you. In this, likewise, there is no doubt.

—*Bahá'u'lláh*

8

O maidservant of God! . . . Never lose thy trust in God. Be thou ever hopeful, for the bounties of God never cease to flow upon man. If viewed from one perspective they seem to decrease, but from another they are full and complete. Man is under all conditions immersed in a sea of God's blessings. Therefore, be thou not hopeless under any circumstances, but rather be firm in thy hope.

—*'Abdu'l-Bahá*

Unity

1

The earth is but one country, and mankind its citizens.

—*Bahá'u'lláh*

2

O my God! O my God! Unite the hearts of Thy servants, and reveal to them Thy great purpose. May they follow Thy commandments and abide in Thy law. Help them, O God, in their endeavor, and grant them strength to serve Thee. O God! Leave them not to themselves, but guide their steps by the light of Thy knowledge, and cheer their hearts by Thy love. Verily, Thou art their Helper and their Lord.

—*Bahá'u'lláh*

3

O thou that hast remembered Me! The most grievous veil hath shut out the peoples of the earth from His glory, and hindered them from hearkening to His call. God grant that the light of unity may envelop the whole earth, and that the seal, "the Kingdom is God's," may be stamped upon the brow of all its peoples.

—*Bahá'u'lláh*

4

The utterance of God is a lamp, whose light is these words: Ye are the fruits of one tree, and the leaves of one branch. Deal ye one with another with the utmost love and harmony, with friendliness and fellowship. He Who is the Daystar of Truth beareth Me witness! So powerful is the light of unity that it can illuminate the whole earth. The one true God, He Who knoweth all things, Himself testifieth to the truth of these words.

—*Bahá'u'lláh*

5

They that are endued with sincerity and faithfulness should associate with all the peoples and kindreds of the earth with joy and radiance, inasmuch as consorting with people hath promoted and will continue to promote unity and concord, which in turn are conducive to the maintenance of order in the world and to the regeneration of nations. Blessed are such as hold fast to the cord of kindliness and tender mercy and are free from animosity and hatred.

—*Bahá'u'lláh*

6

It behooveth thee to consecrate thyself to the Will of God. Whatsoever hath been revealed in His Tablets is but a reflection of His Will. So complete must be thy consecration, that every trace of worldly desire will be washed from thine heart. This is the meaning of true unity.

—*Bahá'u'lláh*

7

My hope is that all the handmaids of God in that region will unite like unto the waves of one unending sea; for although blown about as the wind listeth, these are separate in themselves, yet in truth are they all at one with the boundless deep.

How good it is if the friends be as close as sheaves of light, if they stand together side by side in a firm unbroken line. For now have the rays of reality from the Sun of the world of existence, united in adoration all the worshippers of this light; and these rays have, through infinite grace, gathered all peoples together within this wide-spreading shelter; therefore must all souls become as one soul, and all hearts as one heart. Let all be set free from the multiple identities that were born of passion and desire, and in the oneness of their love for God find a new way of life.

—*'Abdu'l-Bahá*

8

It is the desire of the Lord God that the loved ones of God and the handmaids of the Merciful in the West* should come closer together in harmony and unity as day followeth day . . . This matter is of the utmost importance; this is the magnet that draweth down the confirmations of God. If once the beauty of the unity of the friends—this Divine Beloved—be decked in the adornments of the Abhá Kingdom,† it is certain that within a very short time those countries will become the Paradise of the All-Glorious, and that out of the west the splendors of unity will cast their bright rays over all the earth.

—'Abdu'l-Bahá

9

O my God! O my God! Verily, these are servants at the threshold of Thy mercy, and maidservants at the door of Thy oneness. Verily, they have gathered in this temple to turn to Thy face of glory, holding to the hem of Thy garment and to Thy singleness, seeking Thy good pleasure and ascent into Thy Kingdom. They receive

---

* Women living in the Western hemisphere.

† *The Most Glorious Kingdom:* the spiritual world beyond this world.

effulgence from the Sun of Reality in this glorious century, and they long for Thy goodwill in all great affairs. O Lord! Illumine their sight with a vision of Thy signs and riches, and quicken their ears with hearkening to Thy Word. Render their hearts replete with Thy love, and gladden their spirits with Thy meeting. Deign to bestow upon them spiritual good in Thine earth and heaven, and make them signs of unity among Thy servants in order that the real unity may appear and all may become one in Thy Cause and Kingdom. Verily, Thou art the Generous. Verily, Thou art the Mighty, the Spiritual. Thou art the Merciful, the Clement.

—'Abdu'l-Bahá

10

O my God! O my God! Verily, I invoke Thee and supplicate before Thy threshold, asking Thee that all Thy mercies may descend upon these souls. Specialize them for Thy favor and Thy truth.

O Lord! Unite and bind together the hearts, join in accord all the souls, and exhilarate the spirits through the signs of Thy sanctity and oneness. O Lord! Make these faces radiant through the light of Thy oneness. Strengthen the loins of Thy servants in the service of Thy kingdom.

O Lord, Thou possessor of infinite mercy! O Lord of forgiveness and pardon! Forgive our sins, pardon our shortcomings, and cause us to turn to the kingdom of Thy clemency, invoking the kingdom of might and power, humble at Thy shrine and submissive before the glory of Thine evidences.

O Lord God! Make us as waves of the sea, as flowers of the garden, united, agreed through the bounties of Thy love. O Lord! Dilate the breasts through the signs of Thy oneness, and make all mankind as stars shining from the same height of glory, as perfect fruits growing upon Thy tree of life.

Verily, Thou art the Almighty, the Self-Subsistent, the Giver, the Forgiving, the Pardoner, the Omniscient, the One Creator.

—'Abdu'l-Bahá

11

Through your endeavors, through your heavenly morals, through your devoted efforts a perfect bond of unity and love may be established between the East and the West so that the bestowals of God may descend upon all and that all may be seen to be the parts of the same tree—the great tree of the human family. For mankind may be likened to the branches, leaves, blossoms and fruit of that tree.

The favors of God are unending, limitless. Infinite bounties have encompassed the world. We must emulate the bounties of God, and just as each one of them—the bounty of life, for instance—surrounds and encompasses all, so likewise must we be connected and blended together until each part shall become the expression of the whole.

—'Abdu'l-Bahá

12

May you all be united, may you be agreed, may you serve the solidarity of mankind. May you be well-wishers of all humanity. May you be assistants of every poor one. May you be nurses for the sick. May you be sources of comfort to the broken in heart. May you be a refuge for the wanderer. May you be a source of courage to the affrighted one. Thus, through the favor and assistance of God may the standard of the happiness of humanity be held aloft in the center of the world and the ensign of universal agreement be unfurled.

—'Abdu'l-Bahá

13

Now is the time for the lovers of God to raise high the banners of unity, to intone, in the assemblages of the world, the verses of friendship and love and to demonstrate to all that the grace of God is one. Thus will the tabernacles of holiness be upraised on the summits of the earth, gathering all peoples into the protective shadow of the Word of Oneness. This great bounty will dawn over the world at the time when the lovers of God shall arise to carry out His Teachings, and to scatter far and wide the fresh, sweet scents of universal love.

—'Abdu'l-Bahá

14

O Thou kind Lord! O Thou Who art generous and merciful! We are the servants of Thy threshold and are gathered beneath the sheltering shadow of Thy divine unity. The sun of Thy mercy is shining upon all, and the clouds of Thy bounty shower upon all. Thy gifts encompass all, Thy loving providence sustains all, Thy protection overshadows all, and the glances of Thy favor are cast upon all. O Lord! Grant Thine infinite bestowals, and let the light of Thy guidance shine. Illumine the eyes, gladden the hearts with abiding joy. Confer a new spirit upon all people and bestow upon them eternal life. Unlock the gates of true understanding and let the light of faith shine resplendent. Gather all people beneath the shadow of Thy bounty and cause them to unite in harmony, so that they may become as the rays of one sun, as the waves of one ocean, and as the fruit of one tree. May they drink from the same fountain. May they be refreshed by the same breeze. May they receive illumination from the same source of light. Thou art the Giver, the Merciful, the Omnipotent.

—*'Abdu'l-Bahá*

Wisdom

1

Be ye guided by wisdom in all your doings, and cleave ye tenaciously unto it. Please God ye may all be strengthened to carry out that which is the Will of God, and may be graciously assisted to appreciate the rank conferred upon such of His loved ones as have arisen to serve Him and magnify His name. Upon them be the glory of God, the glory of all that is in the heavens and all that is on the earth, and the glory of the inmates of the most exalted Paradise, the heaven of heavens.

—Bahá'u'lláh

2

Glory be to Thee, Thou in Whose hand are the heaven of omnipotence and the kingdom of creation. Thou doest, by Thy sovereignty, what Thou willest, and ordainest, through the power of Thy might, what Thou pleasest. From eternity Thou hast been exalted above the praise of all created things, and wilt to eternity remain far above the glorification of any one of Thy creatures. Existence itself testifieth to its non-existence when face to face with the manifold revelations of Thy transcendent oneness, and every created thing confesseth, by its very nature, its nothingness when compared with the sacred splendors of the light of Thy unity. Thou hast, in Thyself, been independent of any one besides Thee and rich enough, in Thine own essence, to dispense with any one except Thy Self. Every description by which they who adore Thy unity describe Thee, and every praise wherewith they who are devoted unto Thee praise Thee, are but the traces of the pen which the fingers of Thy strength and power have set in motion—fingers whose movement is controlled by the arm of Thy decree—the arm itself animated by the potency of Thy might.

Thy glory beareth me witness! How can I, aware as I am of this truth, hope to befittingly make mention of Thee and celebrate Thy praise? Howsoever I describe Thee, whichever of Thy virtues I recount, I cannot but blush and feel ashamed of what my tongue hath uttered or my pen written.

The quintessence of knowledge, O my Lord, proclaimeth its powerlessness to know Thee, and perplexity, in its very soul, confesseth its bewilderment in the face of the revelations of Thy sovereign might, and remembrance, in its inmost spirit, acknowledgeth its forgetfulness and effacement before the manifestations of Thy signs and the evidences of Thy praise. What, then, can this poor creature hope to achieve, and to what cord must this wretched soul cling?

I beseech Thee, O Thou Who art the Lord of the worlds, and the Beloved of such as have recognized Thee, and the Desire of all that are in heaven and on earth, by Thy Name through which the cry of every suppliant hath ascended into the heaven of Thy transcendent holiness, through which every seeker hath soared to the sublimities of Thy unity and grandeur, through which the imperfect have been perfected, and the abased exalted, and the tongue of every stammerer unloosed, and the sick made whole, and whatever was unworthy of Thy highness and beseemed not Thy greatness and Thy sovereignty made acceptable unto Thee—I beseech Thee to aid us by Thine invisible hosts and by a company of the angels of Thy Cause. Do Thou, then, accept the works we have performed for love of Thee, and for the sake of Thy pleasure. Cast us not away, O my God, from the door of Thy mercy, and break not our hopes in the wonders of Thy grace and favors.

Our limbs, our members, O my Lord, bear witness to Thy unity and oneness. Send down upon us Thy strength and power, that we may become steadfast in Thy Faith and may aid Thee among

Thy servants. Illumine our eyes, O my Lord, with the effulgence of Thy beauty, and enlighten our hearts with the splendors of Thy knowledge and wisdom. Write us up, then, with those who have fulfilled their pledge to Thy Covenant in Thy days, and who, through their love for Thee, have detached themselves from the world and all that is therein.

Powerful art Thou to do what Thou pleasest. No God is there beside Thee, the All-Powerful, the Omniscient, the Supreme Ruler, the Help in Peril, the Self-Subsisting.

—Bahá'u'lláh

3

Cast away, in My name that transcendeth all other names, the things ye possess, and immerse yourselves in this Ocean* in whose depths lay hidden the pearls of wisdom and of utterance, an ocean that surgeth in My name, the All-Merciful.

—Bahá'u'lláh

4

Turn not away thine eyes from the matchless wine of the immortal Beloved, and open them not to foul and mortal dregs. Take from the hands of the divine Cupbearer the chalice of immortal

---

* The Revelation of Bahá'u'lláh.

life, that all wisdom may be thine, and that thou mayest hearken unto the mystic voice calling from the realm of the invisible.

—*Bahá'u'lláh*

5

The handmaids of God must rise to such a station that they will, by themselves and unaided, comprehend . . . inner meanings, and be able to expound at full length every single word; a station where, out of the truth of their inmost hearts, a spring of wisdom will well up, and jet forth even as a fountain that leapeth from its own original source.

—*'Abdu'l-Bahá*

Notes

Assistance

1. *Prayers and Meditations,* pp. 163–64.
2. Ibid., p. 101.
3. *The Promulgation of Universal Peace,* pp. 385–86
4. Ibid., p. 646.
5. *Bahá'í Prayers,* pp. 56–57.

Certitude

1. *Prayers and Meditations,* pp. 111–12.
2. *The Summons of the Lord of Hosts,* no. 5.14.
3. *Prayers and Meditations,* pp. 283–84.
4. Ibid., pp. 249–50.
5. *The Compilation of Compilations,* 2:2186.
6. *Bahá'í Prayers,* p. 253.
7. *Selections from the Writings of 'Abdu'l-Bahá,* no. 10.1–2.

Courage

1. *Tablets of Bahá'u'lláh,* p. 156.
2. *The Compilation of Compilations,* 2:2100.
3. Ibid., 2:2187.
4. *Paris Talks,* no. 6.12.
5. Ibid., no. 32.14–15.

6. *Selections from the Writings of 'Abdu'l-Bahá*, no. 179.1.

7. Ibid., no. 216.1.

8. *Bahíyyih Khánum: The Greatest Holy Leaf,* p. 100.

Detachment

1. *Bahá'í Prayers*, pp. 246–47.

2. *The Summons of the Lord of Hosts*, no. 1.185.

3. *Bahá'í Prayers*, pp. 55–56.

4. *Selections from the Writings of 'Abdu'l-Bahá*, no. 8.6.

5. Ibid., no. 38.2.

6. Ibid., no. 53.2.

7. Ibid., no. 146.8–11.

8. *Bahá'í Prayers*, pp. 175–76.

Education and Training of Children

1. *Selections from the Writings of 'Abdu'l-Bahá*, no. 106.1–2.

2. Ibid., no. 115.2–4.

3. *The Compilation of Compilations,* 1:610.

4. *Paris Talks*, no. 50.8–10.

5. *The Compilation of Compilations,* 2:2133.

6. *Divine Philosophy*, p. 83

7. *Lights of Guidance*, no. 2084.

Equality

1. *The Compilation of Compilations,* 2:2094.
2. Ibid., 2:2145.
3. Ibid., 2:2145.
4. *Selections from the Writings of 'Abdu'l-Bahá,* no. 227.18.
5. *The Promulgation of Universal Peace,* pp. 102–5.
6. Ibid., p. 106.
7. Ibid., pp. 184–85.
8. Ibid., p. 253.
9. *Paris Talks,* no. 40.33.
10. *The Compilation of Compilations,* 2:2177.
11. *The Promulgation of Universal Peace,* pp. 242–43.
12. *Paris Talks,* no. 59.5.
13. *Selections from the Writings of 'Abdu'l-Bahá,* no. 38.3.
14. *The Compilation of Compilations,* 2:2121.

Family

1. *Tablets of Bahá'u'lláh,* p. 156.
2. *Bahá'í Prayers,* pp. 62–63.
3. *The Promulgation of Universal Peace,* pp. 232–33.
4. Ibid., p. 217.

HUSBANDS
5. *Selections from the Writings of 'Abdu'l-Bahá,* no. 90.1–4.

INFANTS
6. *Bahá'í Prayers,* pp. 32–33.
7. Ibid., p. 33.
8. Ibid., pp. 33–34.

CHILDREN
9. *Bahá'í Prayers,* p. 27.
10. Ibid., p. 28.
11. Ibid., p. 28.

Daughters
12. *Bahá'í Prayers for Women,* p. 9.

PARENTS
13. *Tablets of Bahá'u'lláh,* pp. 24–25.
14. *The Compilation of Compilations,* 1:824.
15. *Bahá'í Prayers,* pp. 63–64.
16. *Selections from the Writings of the Báb,* 3:22:1.

Forgiveness

1. *Prayers and Meditations,* pp. 166–67.
2. Ibid., pp. 245–47.
3. *Gleanings,* no. 138.5.
4. *Bahá'í Prayers,* pp. 78–79.
5. Ibid., p. 80.
6. Ibid., pp. 130–31.
7. Ibid., pp. 82–83.

Grace

1. *Prayers and Meditations,* p. 30.
2. Ibid., pp. 157–59.
3. *Selections from the Writings of 'Abdu'l-Bahá,* no. 2.6–9.
4. Ibid., no. 2.10–11.
5. Ibid., no. 201.1.

The Greatness of this Day

1. *Tablets of Bahá'u'lláh,* pp. 254–55.
2. Ibid., pp. 255–56.
3. *Women: Extracts from the Writings of Bahá'u'lláh, 'Abdu'l-Bahá, Shoghi Effendi, and the Universal House of Justice,* no. 6.
4. *Selections from the Writings of 'Abdu'l-Bahá,* no. 73.4–7.
5. *The Compilation of Compilations,* 2:2189.
6. *The Promulgation of Universal Peace,* p. 474.

Healing

1. *Bahá'í Prayers,* pp. 99–100.
2. The Hidden Words, Persian, no. 32.
3. *Bahá'í Prayers,* pp. 95–96.
4. Ibid., p. 96.
5. *Prayers and Meditations,* pp. 102–3.
6. *Bahá'í Prayers,* pp. 97–99.
7. *Selections from the Writings of 'Abdu'l-Bahá,* no. 139.7–8.

8. Ibid., no. 22.1.
9. Ibid., no. 133.1–3.

Loss of a Loved One
1. *Bahá'í Prayers,* pp. 37–38.
2. Ibid., p. 41.
3. Ibid., pp. 41–42.

LOSS OF A HUSBAND
4. *Selections from the Writings of 'Abdu'l-Bahá,* no. 165.4.

LOSS OF A SON
5. Ibid., no. 171.1–3.

LOSS OF A FEMALE RELATIVE OR FRIEND
6. *Bahá'í Prayers,* pp. 43–44.
7. Ibid., pp. 44–45.
8. Ibid., pp. 45–46.

Love
1. *Gleanings,* no. 153.5.
2. *Prayers and Meditations,* pp. 37–39.
3. Ibid., pp. 56–57.
4. Ibid., p. 145.
5. The Hidden Words, Arabic, no. 5.
6. *Selections from the Writings of 'Abdu'l-Bahá,* no. 12.1.
7. Ibid., no. 1.7.
8. Ibid., no. 174.2–4.

Marriage

1. *Bahá'í Prayers*, p. 120.
2. Ibid., p. 121.
3. *Selections from the Writings of 'Abdu'l-Bahá*, no. 92.1–3.
4. Ibid., no. 84.3–4.
5. Ibid., no. 87.2.
6. Ibid., no. 86.1–2.

Mercy

1. *Gleanings*, no. 27.6.
2. Ibid., no. 5.1.
3. *Bahá'í Prayers*, pp. 244–45.
4. *Prayers and Meditations*, pp. 4–5.
5. *Bahá'í Prayers*, pp. 240–41.
6. *Selections from the Writings of 'Abdu'l-Bahá*, no. 2.4–5.
7. *Paris Talks*, no. 5.11.
8. Ibid., no. 9.24–25.

Morning

1. *Bahá'í Prayers*, p. 124.
2. Ibid., pp. 123–24.
3. *Tablets of Bahá'u'lláh*, p. 138.
4. *Selections from the Writings of 'Abdu'l-Bahá*, no. 8.1–2.
5. *The Compilation of Compilations*, 1:795.

Mothers

1. *Selections from the Writings of 'Abdu'l-Bahá*, no. 95.2.
2. Ibid., no. 96.1–2.
3. Ibid., no. 113.1–3.
4. Ibid., no. 114.1.
5. Ibid., no. 95.1.
6. *Lights of Guidance,* no. 2120.

EXPECTANT MOTHERS
7. *Bahá'í Prayers,* pp. 249–50.

Nearness to God

1. *Gleanings,* no. 93.5.
2. *Prayers and Meditations,* pp. 78–79.
3. *Bahá'í Prayers,* p. 241–42.
4. *Gleanings,* no. 68.5–6.
5. *Bahá'í Prayers,* p. 77–78.
6. *Selections from the Writings of 'Abdu'l-Bahá*, no. 155.6.
7. *Bahá'í Prayers,* pp. 248–49.
8. Ibid., pp. 178–79.
9. Ibid., pp. 132–33.

Patience

1. *Prayers and Meditations,* p. 166.
2. *Gleanings,* no. 134.2.
3. Ibid., no. 114.18.
4. The Hidden Words, Arabic, no. 48.

5. *The Promulgation of Universal Peace,* p. 384.
6. *Bahíyyih <u>Kh</u>ánum: The Greatest Holy Leaf,* p. 97.
7. Ibid., p. 150.

Peace
1. *Gleanings,* no. 4.1.
2. *The Compilation of Compilations,* 2:1573.
3. *Gleanings,* no. 92.3.
4. *The Promulgation of Universal Peace,* pp. 243–44.
5. Ibid., p. 186.
6. *Selections from the Writings of 'Abdu'l-Bahá,* no. 201.2.
7. *The Promulgation of Universal Peace,* p. 530.
8. Ibid., pp. 149–50.
9. *Bahá'í Prayers,* pp. 113–15.
10. *The Compilation of Compilations,* 2:1615.
11. *Lights of Guidance,* no. 2089.
12. *Peace: More than an End to War,* pp. 14–15.
13. *Lights of Guidance,* no. 2090.

Praise
1. *Epistle to the Son of the Wolf,* p. 25–26.
2. *Women: Extracts from the Writings of Bahá'u'lláh, 'Abdu'l-Bahá, Shoghi Effendi, and the Universal House of Justice,* no. 53.
3. *The Compilation of Compilations,* 2:2184.

4. *Prayers and Meditations,* p. 55–56.
5. Ibid., pp. 113–15.
6. *Selections from the Writings of 'Abdu'l-Bahá,* no. 153.1.
7. *Bahíyyih Khánum: The Greatest Holy Leaf,* p. 156.

Protection

1. *Bahá'í Prayers,* pp. 146–47.
2. *Prayers and Meditations,* pp. 126–27.
3. *Bahá'í Prayers,* pp. 247–48.
4. *Prayers and Meditations,* p. 142.
5. *Bahá'í Prayers,* pp. 242–43.

Qualities of Women

1. *Women: Extracts from the Writings of Bahá'u'lláh, 'Abdu'l-Bahá, Shoghi Effendi, and the Universal House of Justice,* no. 7.
2. *The Compilation of Compilations,* 2:2095.
3. Ibid., no. 2185.
4. *Lights of Guidance,* no. 749.
5. *Women: Extracts from the Writings of Bahá'u'lláh, 'Abdu'l-Bahá, Shoghi Effendi, and the Universal House of Justice,* no. 8.
6. *The Compilation of Compilations,* 2:2168.
7. *The Promulgation of Universal Peace,* p. 396.
8. *'Abdu'l-Bahá in London,* pp. 102–3.
9. *Paris Talks,* no. 50.6.

10. *Lights of Guidance,* no. 2079.
11. *The Compilation of Compilations,* 1:846.
12. *Selections from the Writings of 'Abdu'l-Bahá,*
    no. 93.1–2.

Service

1. *Gleanings,* no. 144.2–3.
2. *Tablets of Bahá'u'lláh,* pp. 116–17.
3. *Gleanings,* no. 130.1.
4. *Selections from the Writings of 'Abdu'l-Bahá,* no.
    1.7.
5. Ibid., no. 80.1.
6. Ibid., no. 218.7.
7. Ibid., no. 236.4.

Steadfastness

1. *Prayers and Meditations,* pp. 77–78.
2. *Gleanings,* no. 134.3.
3. *Bahá'í Prayers,* pp. 185–86.
4. *Prayers and Meditations,* pp. 188–89.
5. *Bahá'í Prayers,* p. 71.
6. Ibid., p. 191.
7. *Bahíyyih <u>Kh</u>ánum: The Greatest Holy Leaf,* p. 148.

Suffering and Difficulties

1. *Prayers and Meditations,* pp. 231–32.
2. *Bahá'í Prayers,* p. 220.
3. Ibid., pp. 223–24.

4. *Prayers and Meditations,* pp. 15–16.
5. *Bahá'í Prayers,* p. 226.
6. *Selections from the Writings of 'Abdu'l-Bahá,* no. 91.1.
7. Ibid., no. 141.4–6.
8. Ibid., no. 150.1–4.
9. Ibid., no. 155.2–4.
10. *Baḥíyyih Khánum: The Greatest Holy Leaf,* pp. 183–84.

Trust in God
1. *Bahá'í Prayers,* p. 224–25.
2. *Gleanings,* no. 128.9.
3. Ibid., no. 136.4.
4. *Gems of Divine Mysteries,* ¶83.
5. *Tablets of Bahá'u'lláh,* p. 155.
6. Ibid., pp. 189–90.
7. *The Compilation of Compilations,* 1:334.
8. *Selections from the Writings of 'Abdu'l-Bahá,* no. 178.1.

Unity
1. *Gleanings,* no. 117.1.
2. *Bahá'í Prayers,* p. 238.
3. *Gleanings,* no. 7.3.
4. Ibid., no. 132.3.
5. *Tablets of Bahá'u'lláh,* p. 36.
6. *Gleanings,* no. 160.3.

7. *Selections from the Writings of 'Abdu'l-Bahá*, no. 36.2–3.

8. Ibid., no. 41.2

9. *The Promulgation of Universal Peace*, p. 270.

10. *Bahá'í Prayers*, pp. 238–39.

11. *The Promulgation of Universal Peace*, p. 21.

12. Ibid., p. 599.

13. *Selections from the Writings of 'Abdu'l-Bahá*, no. 7.3.

14. *The Promulgation of Universal Peace*, p. 160.

Wisdom

1. *Gleanings*, no. 96.4.

2. *Prayers and Meditations*, pp. 172–74.

3. *Gleanings*, no. 14.16.

4. The Hidden Words, Persian, no. 62.

5. *Selections from the Writings of 'Abdu'l-Bahá*, no. 142.9.

Alphabetical Index to First Lines of Prayers and Meditations

225

Bahá'í

PUBLISHING

and the Bahá'í Faith

Bahá'í Publishing produces books based on the teachings of the Bahá'í Faith. Founded over 160 years ago, the Bahá'í Faith has spread to some 235 nations and territories and is now accepted by more than five million people. The word "Bahá'í" means "follower of Bahá'u'lláh." Bahá'u'lláh, the founder of the Bahá'í Faith, asserted that he is the Messenger of God for all of humanity in this day. The cornerstone of his teachings is the establishment of the spiritual unity of humankind, which will be achieved by personal transformation and the application of clearly identified spiritual principles. Bahá'ís also believe that there is but one religion and that all the Messengers of God—among them Abraham, Zoroaster, Moses, Krishna, Buddha, Jesus, and Muḥammad—have progressively revealed its nature. Together, the world's great religions are expressions of a single, unfolding divine plan. Human beings, not God's Messengers, are the source of religious divisions, prejudices, and hatreds.

The Bahá'í Faith is not a sect or denomination of another religion, nor is it a cult or a social movement. Rather, it is a globally recognized independent world religion founded on new books of scripture revealed by Bahá'u'lláh.

Bahá'í Publishing is an imprint of the National Spiritual Assembly of the Bahá'ís of the United States.

For more information about the Bahá'í Faith,
or to contact Bahá'ís near you, visit
http://www.bahai.us/
or call
1-800-22-UNITE

Other Books Available from Bahá'í Publishing

IN THE GLORY OF THE FATHER
THE BAHÁ'Í FAITH AND CHRISTIANITY
by Brian Lepard
$17.00 U.S. / $19.00 CAN
Trade paper
ISBN 13: 978-1-931847-34-6
ISBN 10: 1-931847-34-7

Author Brian Lepard draws upon his childhood religious experiences and his study of the Bible and other holy books to recount his spiritual journey and discovery of the Bahá'í Faith. He describes in some detail the lives of the central figures of the Bahá'í Faith: the Báb, Who heralded the coming of Bahá'u'lláh; Bahá'u'lláh, the Prophet-Founder of the Bahá'í Faith; 'Abdu'l-Bahá, the son and successor of Bahá'u'lláh; and more. Lepard discusses the similarities between Bahá'í and Christian views of the station of Jesus Christ, biblical interpretation, and the nature of God, and discusses whether it is possible to build the Kingdom of God on earth and how biblical prophecy has been fulfilled through the coming of Bahá'u'lláh.

This book is aimed at Christian readers who have heard of the Bahá'í Faith and are interested in learning more about the relationship between the teachings of Christianity and the teachings of the Bahá'í Faith.

THE PEN OF GLORY
SELECTED WORKS OF BAHÁ'U'LLÁH
by Bahá'u'lláh
$12.00 U.S. / $14.00 CAN
Trade paper
ISBN 13: 978-1-931847-55-1
ISBN 10: 1-931847-55-X

The Pen of Glory: Selected Works of Bahá'u'lláh is a compilation of several works from the writings of Bahá'u'lláh, the Prophet-Founder of the Bahá'í Faith, responding to questions posed by people of other faiths. These selections are unique because they were written in response to specific questions from people wishing to know more about the principles and teachings of the Bahá'í Faith. Because these people came from various religious backgrounds, their questions elicited responses that provide the reader with a broad understanding of the central tenets of the Bahá'í Faith. In each of the works included in the volume, Bahá'u'lláh responds to the question of a seeker and then expounds on various related spiritual themes. In doing so, He has provided a collection of writings of enduring and far-reaching significance that remains applicable to the questions of religious seekers today.

ADAM'S WISH
UNKNOWN POETRY OF ṬÁHIRIH
by John S. Hatcher and *Amrollah Hemmat*
$18.00 U.S. / $20.00 CAN
Trade paper
ISBN 13: 978-1-931847-61-2
ISBN 10: 1-931847-61-4

A priceless collection of previously unpublished poems by the renowned nineteenth-century poetess Ṭáhirih. Many of the poems were either thought to be lost or remained untranslated and largely unknown. They are provided here both in their original calligraphy and in English. Many of the poems relate to Ṭáhirih's spiritual beliefs. She often refers to Adam, the first Prophet of God, and to the Prophets of the past to reveal her insights into the process by which God empowers His Messengers to educate humanity. It is through this process that we are able to see the fulfillment of the wish of Adam and all the Prophets of the past to witness the day when humanity will reach its full spiritual potential. Ṭáhirih announces that the long awaited day has now come, and her poetry is a celebration of love for God and His Prophets.

To view our complete catalog,
please visit http://books.bahai.us